Nick Cotton

cycling traffic-free
Home Counties

Allan
PUBLISHING

ee: Home Counties

010

0 3435 8

shing Ltd 2010

Allan Publishing

Allan Publishing Ltd, Hersham, Surrey KT12 4RG.
d by Ian Allan Printing Ltd, Hersham, Surrey KT12 4RG.

Publishing website at www.ianallanpublishing.com

United States of America and Canada by BookMasters Distribution

CONTENTS

THE MAIN ROUTES

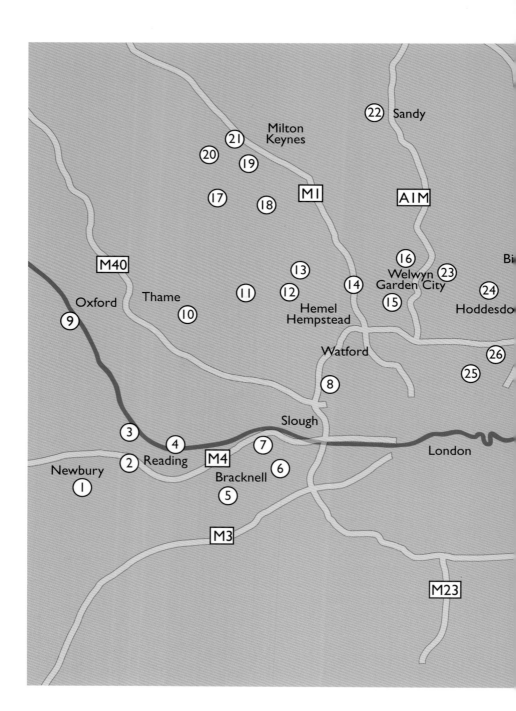

INTRODUCTION

More and more people are realising that cycling is good for both health and well-being. The government has started showing a real interest in promoting cycling as a way of solving transport problems and the National Cycle Network has had a positive effect, changing lifestyles and people's choice of transport. However, vehicle numbers are still increasing which means that even minor lanes can become busy with traffic – you can very rarely be guaranteed to find the safety, peace and quiet that are the essential ingredients of a family bike ride on the road network.

This book describes 30 routes, many of them easy and waymarked, where you can cycle free from traffic and gives details about where to find information about other rides.

OTHER ROUTES IN BRIEF

In addition to the 30 main rides featured in the book there are several routes in the area which are worth a brief mention:

LONDON

Grand Union Canal

As mentioned in Ride 8, very little of the Grand Union Canal between Paddington and Uxbridge offers enjoyable recreational cycling with the exception of Kensal Rise (Sainsbury's) west to Horsenden Hill for about 5 miles. The rest is at times narrow, overgrown, rough and bumpy or interrupted by a series of anti-motorbike barriers or a combination of all of these. Things can only get better!

Parkland Walk and Finsbury Park

A short railway path from Highgate leads to a circuit of Finsbury Park.

Victoria Park, Hackney

There is a circuit around the perimeter of the park.

The Greenway from Stratford to Beckton

An old railway line in East London running east from the Olympic Site in Stratford (just east of Victoria Park) to the A1020 to the north of London City Airport.

BERKSHIRE

Jubilee River

National Cycle Network Route 61 runs alongside the recently created Jubilee River from just east of Maidenhead to Ditton Park, to the south of Slough. Visit www.sustrans.org.uk and put 'Jubilee River' in the 'Search' box.

Slough Arm

A 5-mile branch of the Grand Union Canal from Slough to Yiewsley (south of Uxbridge). At times it is quite narrow.

OXFORDSHIRE

Didcot and Abingdon

There are several short traffic-free trails near these two towns, some of which form part of National Cycle Network Route 6. Visit www.sustrans.org.uk and put 'Didcot' or 'Abingdon' in the 'Search' box

Oxford Canal

Runs north from the River Thames in central Oxford through to Kidlington and beyond. Much of it is quite narrow and bumpy although there are also some smoother sections. Mountain bikes with suspension recommended.

Ridgeway/Icknield Way

Parts of this offer reasonably easy mountain biking on dry summer days. There is a long bridleway section near to Chinnor and Watlington.

BUCKINGHAMSHIRE

Wendover and Aylesbury Arms of the Grand Union Canal

Both these spurs off the main canal have towpaths although the surface tends to be rough so mountain bikes with suspension are recommended.

HERTFORDSHIRE

Ebury Way

A 3-mile railway path from Batchworth (Rickmansworth) to Watford. To download a map go to: www.groundwork-herts.org.uk/upload/documents/webpage/Ebury_Way.pdf

Lee Valley

Rides 24 & 25 describe the Lee Navigation towpath between London and Hertford but there are several other routes in the linear park. See www.leevalleypark.org.uk and follow links to 'Cycling' or www.waterscape.com

Stort Navigation

The towpath runs for 14 miles from Bishop's Stortford southwest to the junction of the Stort Navigation with the Lee Navigation near Roydon. Mountain bikes with suspension are recommended.

TOURIST INFORMATION CENTRES

Bedfordshire
Ampthill	08542 304 040
Bedford	01234 221 712
Biggleswade	08452 304040
Dunstable	01582 890 270
Luton	01582 401 579
Sandy	01767 682 728

Berkshire
Ashford	01233 629165
Bracknell	01344 354409
Maidenhead	01628 796502
Newbury	01635 30267
Windsor	01753 743 900

Buckinghamshire
Aylesbury	01296 330 559
Buckingham	01280 823020
High Wycombe	01494 421 892
Marlow	01628 483597
Princes Risborough	01844 274 795
Wendover	01296 696759

Essex
Braintree	01376 550 066
Brentwood	01277 200300
Clacton-on-Sea	01255 686 633
Colchester	01206 282 920
Harwich	01255 506139
Maldon	01621 856503
Saffron Walden	01799 510444
Southend-on-Sea	01702 215 120
Waltham Abbey	01992 652 295
Walton-on-the-Naze	01255 675542

Hertfordshire
Baldock	01438 737333
Birchanger Green	01279 508656
Bishop's Stortford	01279 655831
Borehamwood	0208 207 7496
Buntingford	01763 272689
Harpenden	01582 768278
Hemel Hempstead	01442 234 222
Hertford	01992 584 322
Hitchin	01438 737333
Hoddesdon	01438 737333
Letchworth	01462 487 868
Rickmansworth	01923 776611
Royston	01438 737333
St Albans	01727 864511
Stevenage	01438 737333
Tring	01442 823347

Oxfordshire
Abingdon	01235 522 711
Banbury	01295 259855
Didcot	01235 813243
Henley	01491 578 034
Oxford	01865 252200
Thame	01844 212834
Wallingford	01491 826 972
Woodstock	01993 813 276

Suffolk
Ipswich	01473 258 070
Woodbridge	01394 382 240

USEFUL WEBSITES

More and more cycling information is being made available on the internet and the better websites are constantly being upgraded. If you are prepared to search for 'Cycling' or 'Cycle routes' on local authority websites you will normally find details of routes and leaflets, some of which you will be able to download and print off at home.

www.sustrans.org.uk

The Sustrans website is being improved year by year and this is often the best place to start on your hunt for cycling information relating to rides close to where you live or where you are going on holiday.

LONDON

www.tfl.gov.uk/roadusers and click on 'Cycling'
www.lcc.org.uk
www.royalparks.org.uk

BEDFORDSHIRE

www.bedford.gov.uk/transport_and_streets/cycling.aspx

BERKSHIRE

www.westberks.gov.uk
(Click on 'Transport & Streets' then 'Transport Policy' then 'Cycling')

BUCKINGHAMSHIRE

www.visitbuckinghamshire.org/site/cycling_in_buckinghamshire
www.buckscc.gov.uk/bcc/transport/cycling.page?

ESSEX

www.essex.gov.uk (Scroll down and click on 'Cycling and Walking' under the 'Travelling' section at the bottom of the left-hand side)

HERTFORDSHIRE

www.hertsdirect.org/atozoflinks/cycling/
www.welhat.gov.uk > Leisure > Cycling and Walking

OXFORDSHIRE

www.oxford.gov.uk > Council Services > Transport > Cycling
www.oxfordshire.gov.uk > Roads and transport > Cycling

SUFFOLK

www.suffolk.gov.uk > Transport and streets > Cycling

WHERE TO CYCLE TRAFFIC-FREE
NORTH AND WEST OF LONDON

In general traffic-free cycling routes can be divided into six categories:

- Dismantled railways
- Forestry Commission routes
- Waterside routes including reservoirs, canals and riverside routes
- London parks and country parks
- Routes created by local authorities, often as part of the National Cycle Network
- The Rights of Way network – byways and bridleways

DISMANTLED RAILWAYS

The vast majority of Britain's railway system was built in the 50 years from 1830 to 1880. After the invention of the car and the development of the road network from the turn of the 20th century onwards, the railways went into decline and in the 1960s many of the lines were closed and the tracks lifted. This was the famous 'Beeching Axe'. It is a great tragedy that Dr Beeching was not a keen leisure cyclist!

Had he set in motion the development of leisure trails along the course of the railways he was so busy closing, then we could boast one of the finest recreational cycling networks in the world.

As it is, many of the railways were sold off in small sections to adjacent landowners and the continuity of long sections of dismantled track was lost. Almost fifty years on, some local authorities have risen to the challenge and created some fine trails along the course of the dismantled railways. Within this book the Phoenix Trail (Ride 10), Nickey Line (Ride 14), Alban Way (Ride 15), Ayot Greenway (Ride 16), Bedford to Sandy (Ride 22), the Cole Green Way (Ride 23) and the Flitch Way (Ride 27) are all good examples.

Dismantled railways make good cycle trails for two reasons: first, the gradients tend to be very gentle, and second, the broad stone base is ideal for creating a smooth, firm surface for bicycles.

FORESTRY COMMISSION LAND

There are two Forestry Commission holdings with waymarked routes in the area covered by this book: Wendover Woods, southeast of Aylesbury (Ride 11) and Rendlesham Forest, northeast of Ipswich (Ride 30).

The woodlands of Bracknell (Ride 5) are owned by the Crown Estate and Epping Forest (Ride 26) by the Corporation of London. The nearest large Forestry Commission woodland is at Thetford. The Forestry Commission website – www.forestry.gov.uk – is an excellent source of information about cycling and mountain biking.

WATERSIDE ROUTES: CANAL TOWPATHS, RIVERSIDE ROUTES AND RESERVOIRS.

The British Waterways Board undertook a national survey of its 2,000 miles of towpath to see what percentage was suitable for cycling. Unfortunately, the results were not very encouraging – only about 10% meet the specified requirements. The rest are too narrow, too rutted, too overgrown or pass under too many low bridges. In certain cases regional water boards have co-ordinated with local authorities to improve the towpaths for all users. It is to be hoped that this collaboration continues and extends throughout the country.

Cycling along canal towpaths can provide plenty of interest – wildlife, barges and locks – and the gradient tends to be flat. However, even the best-quality towpaths are not places to cycle fast as they are often busy with anglers and walkers and it is rare that cycling two abreast is feasible. For more information go to the British Waterways website at www.waterscape.com.

The most important waterways for cycling in the area covered by the book are the Kennet & Avon Canal (Rides 1 and 2), the River Thames (Rides 4 and 9), the Grand Union Canal (Rides 8, 12, 18 and 21) and the Lee Navigation (Rides 24 and 25). Other waterways in the Southeast such as the Basingstoke Canal and the Wey Navigation are covered in another book in the series: *Cycling Traffic Free: South East*. Alton Water (Ride 29) is one of the few reservoirs to the north of London with a cycle trail around it.

LONDON PARKS AND COUNTRY PARKS

Several parks in London have cycle trails – see www.royalparks.org.uk. There is some wonderful cycling on the estate roads of Windsor Great Park (Ride 6); there are several bridleways in Ashridge Estate (Ride 13). There are numerous country parks to the north and west of London. To find out more information it is best to go via the local authority websites and put 'Country Parks' into the 'Search' box. This will then let you see which parks are suitable for cycling.

ROUTES CREATED BY LOCAL AUTHORITIES

By using a mixture of quiet lanes and improved footpaths and bridleways local authorities can signpost and promote a route to make the most of existing networks. These include the route from Windsor to Bray (Ride 7), the trail from Milton Keynes to Winslow (Ride 17) and the route between Colchester and Wivenhoe (Ride 28).

RIGHTS OF WAY NETWORK: THE RIDGEWAY

The Ridgeway is a long distance byway running east from Overton Hill (on the A4 west of Marlborough) to Goring and offers tough challenges for fit cyclists on mountain bikes. These rides are tougher than those along railway paths and canal towpaths and should only be undertaken on mountain bikes (preferably with suspension) after a few dry days in summer. Most of the Ridgeway lies to the west of the area covered by this book but the section from East Ilsley to Goring offers some wonderful views but also some tough climbs. To the east of the Thames the Ridgeway's status changes between footpath (where you are *not* allowed to ride) and bridleway or byway (where you *may* ride). There is a long rideable stretch (on a dry summer's day) in the Watlington/Chinnor area.

OTHER CYCLE ROUTES

If you wish to venture beyond the relatively protected world of cycle trails, there are three choices: buy a guidebook covering mountain bike rides or rides on the lane network, look on websites for leaflets produced by local authorities or devise your own route.

Should you choose the third option, study the relevant Ordnance Survey Landranger map: the yellow roads criss-crossing the countryside represent the

smaller quieter lanes. When cycling off-road you must stay on legal rights of way: it is illegal to cycle on footpaths, but you are allowed to use bridleways, byways open to all traffic (BOATs), and roads used as public paths (RUPPs). These are all marked on Ordnance Survey maps.

Devising routes 'blind' can sometimes be a bit of a hit-or-miss affair, however. Some tracks may turn out to be very muddy and overgrown or no more than an imaginary line across a ploughed field! It often takes several outings to devise the best possible off-road route that starts right from your front door. Expect the riding conditions to change radically from the height of summer to the depths of winter.

EXITS FROM LONDON

The best cycling 'escape routes' from London are along the watercourses of the River Thames and the canals. The Thames can be followed from Putney Bridge southwest to Weybridge; to the east, the Thames can be followed from Greenwich to Erith; the Grand Union Canal starts near Paddington and runs west to Hayes then north through Uxbridge to Rickmansworth and Watford (Ride 8 covers the section north of Denham); to the northeast, the Lee Valley offers an exit to

Waltham Abbey, Ware and Hertford (Rides 24 and 25). The rides along the Thames are covered in another book in the series, *Cycling Traffic Free: South East.*

SUSTRANS & THE NATIONAL CYCLE NETWORK

The National Cycle Network is a linked series of traffic-free paths and traffic-calmed roads being developed right across the United Kingdom, linking town centres and the countryside. Visit Sustrans' website – www.sustrans.org.uk – for more details. In the region covered by this book there is one main National Cycle Network long distance route covered by a map (see the Sustrans website):

London to Oxford (the Thames Valley Cycle Route). Sections of this are covered in the book: through Oxford (Ride 9), through Reading (Ride 4), between Windsor and Bray (Ride 7) and through Windsor Great Park (Ride 7).

THE COUNTRY CODE

- Enjoy the countryside and respect its life and work

- Guard against all risk of fire

- Fasten all gates

- Keep your dogs under close control

- Keep to rights of way across farmland

- Use gates and stiles to cross fences, hedges and walls

- Leave livestock, crops and machinery alone

- Take your litter home

- Help to keep all water clean

- Protect wildlife, plants and trees

- Take special care on country roads

- Make no unnecessary noise

CYCLING TRAFFIC-FREE:
HOME COUNTIES
THE MAIN ROUTES

ROUTE I
Kennet and Avon Canal from Newbury to Aldermaston

Distance: 9 miles one way, 18 miles return.

Map: Ordnance Survey Landranger map 174.

Website: www.waterscape.com/canals-and-rivers/kennet-and-avon-canal

Hills: None.

Surface: Good gravel-based track with some short, rougher sections.

Roads and road crossings: Several road crossings, one of which (Ham Bridge, about 1½ miles east of Newbury) is busy.

Refreshments: Lots of choice in Newbury. Rowbarge pub, Woolhampton. Butt Inn, Tearoom at Visitor Centre, Aldermaston Wharf.

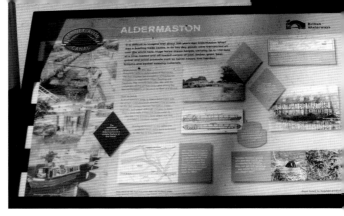

Linking the West Country to London, the Kennet & Avon Canal offers many miles of good towpath cycling both at its western end between Bath and Devizes and, as described in this book in Rides 1 and 2, between Newbury and Reading. The highpoint of the canal lies at Savernake, to the west of Newbury, so the canal is descending down to the Thames as it runs east, parallel with the River Kennet, a river that criss-crosses the canal and ensures that the water level is maintained. The surface of the towpath varies but is generally of quite good standard. Aldermaston Wharf has a small visitor centre and cafe and is the suggested turn-around point, although you could easily continue on to Reading. There are useful train stations close to the canal at several points.

BACKGROUND AND PLACES OF INTEREST
Kennet & Avon Canal
The canal was built in three sections. The first two were river navigations, the Kennet from Reading to Newbury and the Avon from Bath to Bristol both being canalised. Among early 18th-century river navigations the Kennet was one of the most ambitious: between Reading and Newbury 18 locks were necessary in as many miles as the river falls 138ft over that distance. The Kennet section was built between 1718 and 1723.

Starting Points & Parking:
1. Bridge Street, Newbury. The canal passes right through the heart of Newbury (Grid reference SU 471671). There are several car parks in the centre of town although if you live outside Newbury it may be preferable to start further east and cycle into Newbury.

2. Aldermaston Wharf, just off the A340 near its junction with the A4 about 9 miles east of Newbury. There is a car park at the back of the Visitor Centre on Ufton Grove (Grid reference SU 603672).

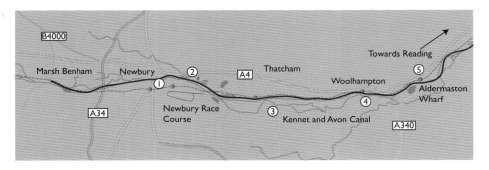

ROUTE INSTRUCTIONS:

East from Newbury

1. Follow the towpath through the centre of Newbury staying close to the canal itself, avoiding diversions alongside the river or via National Cycle Network Route 4 which occasionally takes a different course.
2. The towpath frequently changes sides. About 1½ miles from Newbury, take care crossing the B3421 Hambridge Road.
3. Go out into the country past Thatcham railway station.
4. Go past the Rowbarge pub in Woolhampton.
5. The suggested turnaround point at the east end is at Aldermaston Wharf. However, you may wish to continue towards Reading.

West from Newbury

The canal can be followed for 3 miles west from Newbury as far as Marsh Benham. It is signposted as National Cycle Network Route 4. Beyond this point the towpath quality deteriorates, as NCN 4 leaves the canal and follows lanes to Hungerford.

ROUTE 2
Kennet and Avon Canal from Aldermaston Wharf to Reading

Distance: 11 miles one way, 22 miles return.

Map: Ordnance Survey Landranger map 175.

Website: www.waterscape.com/canals-and-rivers/kennet-and-avon-canal

Hills: None.

Surface: Stone-based tracks with some rougher sections and two short stretches on grass.

Roads and road crossings: Several road crossings. Care should be taken in the centre of Reading.

Refreshments: Butt Inn, Tearoom at the Visitor Centre, Aldermaston Wharf. Cunning Man pub, halfway between Theale and Reading. Lots of choice in Reading.

The second of the two rides exploring the canal takes you right though the centre of Reading to the canal's junction with the Thames. It has a mixture of surfaces including two short sections where it is just grass as it passes through meadows where it was felt that a stone-based path would look out of place. To the east of Theale there is a short section where you are diverted away from the canal – the towpath at this point is rough and muddy and there are stiles to negotiate. The alternative is alongside the noisy M4 for about ½ mile and it is a real relief to get back to the canal and enjoy the peace of the countryside. You need to have your wits about you through the centre of Reading but it is worth the effort as the junction of the canal with the majestic River Thames offers a real sense of destination.

BACKGROUND AND PLACES OF INTEREST

The canal – decline and rebirth

The opening of the Great Western Railway in 1841 was a severe blow to the economic success of the canal, taking away much of its traffic. Its long decline continued through to the Second World War when a large number of concrete bunkers (pill boxes) were built as part of the defence against possible invasion. In 1963, the newly formed British Waterways took over the canal and restoration work began in 1990. Queen Elizabeth officially re-opened the canal.

Starting Points & Parking:

1. Aldermaston Wharf, just off the A340 near its junction with the A4 about 9 miles east of Newbury. There is a car park at the back of the Visitor Centre on Ufton Grove (Grid reference SU 603672).

2. Reading – the canal runs right through Reading and joins the Thames just east of the town centre. There is a free car park near the junction of the canal and the Thames off the roundabout at the western end of the A329/A3290 at Wokingham Waterside Centre on Thames Valley Park Drive (Grid reference SU 736740).

ROUTE INSTRUCTIONS:

1. From the Aldermaston Wharf Visitor Centre turn left along the towpath, with the canal to your right.

2. After 1½ miles there is the first short grass section.

3. Go past Tyle Mill car park and on to the second grass section.

4. Go past the Sheffield Bottom Lock Picnic Area, pass under the M4 then shortly, at a T-junction turn right away from the canal to pass along the south side of the lake close to the motorway. At the next T-junction, with tarmac, at the end of the lake, turn left, signposted 'National Cycle Network Route 4'. After ½ mile, on a sharp right-hand bend, with Dewe Lane to the left, go straight ahead onto a fine gravel track 'NCN 4'.

5. Rejoin the canal and turn right. Go past the Cunning Man pub.

6. After 2 miles, as National Cycle Network Route 4 bears left away from the canal, stay on the towpath. The surface is at first rough but soon improves.

7. Emerge in the town centre by House of Fraser. Cross the road and continue alongside the water following bike signs for 'Wargrave'. At the next bridge turn left then immediately right onto Star Lane. Follow for 1 mile to the canal's junction with the River Thames. If you wish to return to the Thames Valley Park Drive car park (or to join Ride 4 to Sonning) turn right along the Thames.

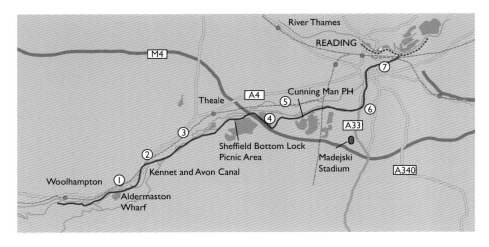

ROUTE 3
Goring to Reading along the Thames Valley

Distance: 8 miles one way, 16 miles return.

Map: Ordnance Survey Landranger map 175.

Hills: Several gentle climbs and one short very steep one.

Surface: Tarmac, stone-based tracks, with some short rougher sections.

Roads and road crossings: Several sections of quiet lanes are used. There is one 100 yard stretch of busy road (the B471 in Whitchurch) where you may prefer to walk.

Refreshments: Lots of choice in Goring. Pub just off the route in Whitchurch (you will have to use a busy road). Lots of choice in Reading just beyond the end of the route.

This is not a cycle trail in the normal sense of the word. It is not a railway path nor a canal towpath nor a waymarked forestry route but nevertheless, in the summer months, it offers a wonderful ride along the broad valley formed by the River Thames with a particularly magical section right by the river just to the east of Goring. Other attractions along the way include the red-brick splendour of Mapledurham House and the hundreds of alpacas at Bozedown Farm all peacefully grazing the lush green fields. At the eastern end of the ride, a quiet residential road (The Warren) takes you close to the centre of Reading but unfortunately there is no safe connection through to the traffic-free paths alongside the Thames. If you are prepared to brave the traffic or walk for about ¼ mile along Church Road and Bridge Street this will give you access to Ride 4 along the Thames to Sonning and a connection to the Kennet & Avon Canal rides. (Rides 1 and 2)

NB This ride will get muddy in winter and after heavy rain. There is also one short steep descent then climb with steps on the section between Goring and Whitchurch so this is not a ride for very young children.

Starting Points & Parking:
1. Goring – the railway station car park, on the southeast edge of town (Grid reference SU 602807).
2. Reading – there is no easy, safe link from the centre of Reading to the start of the trail. There is some parking at the end of the road called 'The Warren', off Church Road just north of the Thames (Grid reference SU 692754).

ROUTE INSTRUCTIONS:

1. Exit Goring railway station car park and turn right on the no through road. After about ½ mile, with an 'Unsuitable for motor vehicles' sign ahead, bear right, signposted 'Bridleway to Whitchurch' 2½.

2. After 300 yards as the tarmac lane swings right, bear left on a concrete track signposted 'No entry' (blue bridleway arrow). Shortly, at a crossroads of tracks, go straight ahead between a house and garage onto a wide concrete path that soon turns to track.

3. The track is at first a bit rough but soon improves for a magical section, climbing through woodland above the River Thames. There is one very steep down then up, where there are steps.

4. Join tarmac and continue straight ahead (Hartslock Farm is down to your right). At the T-junction with the busy B471 turn right downhill for 100 yards then first left onto Hardwick Road signposted 'Goring Heath'. Take care on the B471; you may prefer to walk.

5. Go past the alpacas at Bozedown Farm. As the road swings sharp left uphill continue straight ahead: 'Hardwick Estate, Private Road'. Shortly at a three-way split of tracks take the left-hand, upper track (i.e. NOT 'Private Drive' or 'Hardwick Estate').

6. The track narrows and becomes rougher. At the T-junction with road turn right then shortly on a sharp right-hand bend bear left by a red-brick house with tall chimneys onto a concrete track signposted 'Private Road, Bridlepath only'. Go past Mapledurham House.

7. Ignore turns to right and left, continue in the same direction. The concrete track turns to stone and gravel for ½ mile and ends at a metal barrier. You may wish to turn around here or continue on the quiet road as far as St Peter's Church or even go into Reading itself. If you choose the latter there is a short section on busy roads until you get to the Thames, where you can join a traffic-free path east along the river (on the south side).

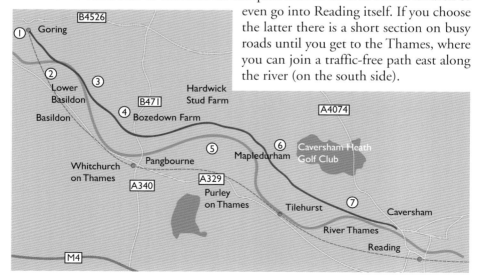

ROUTE 4

Along the Thames from Reading to Sonning

Distance: 2 miles east to Sonning (i.e. 4 miles return) and 2 miles west to Caversham Bridge (also 4 miles return). From its junction with the Thames, it is also possible to follow the Kennet & Avon Canal into the centre of Reading and beyond.

Map: Ordnance Survey Landranger map 175. A leaflet called *Cycling in Reading* shows all the cycle routes and facilities in Reading.

Go to www.reading.gov.uk/cycling for more details.

Website: Reading Borough Council's website is www.reading.gov.uk.

For Reading Cycle Campaign go to: www.readingcyclecampaign.org.uk

Hills: There are no hills.

Surface: Good quality tracks.

Roads and road crossings: There is a very short section on a quiet road if you go to the pub in Sonning.

Refreshments: Lock Tea Gardens just west of Sonning. Bull Inn, Great House Hotel, Sonning. Jolly Angler pub, Fisherman's Cottage pub are just off the route, on the Kennet & Avon canal towpath as you approach Reading centre.

There are few stretches of the Thames west of London where it is possible to ride – this section in and near Reading is one of them. Reading is where the Kennet & Avon Canal joins the Thames, thus linking Bristol to London (via the River Avon and River Thames). It is possible to cycle along the towpath of the canal into the centre of Reading. The town is at an important junction of the National Cycle Network – Route 4 runs through Reading on its way from London to Wales and Route 6 heads north from Reading through the Chiltern Hills to Oxford. You will see one of the attractive Sustrans Millennium Mileposts at the point where Route 4 joins the Thames. Sonning is a fine little village with a good pub.

There are also tea gardens at Sonning Lock, just before the village.

Starting Point & Parking:

There is a free car park east of Reading town centre near the junction of the Kennet & Avon Canal and the River Thames. It is located off the roundabout at the western end of the A329/A3290, where it joins Thames Valley Park Drive. The car park has a 'Wokingham Waterside Centre' sign (Grid reference SU 736740).

ROUTE INSTRUCTIONS

East to Sonning

1. Exit the car park and turn left on the shared-use pavement along Thames Valley Park Drive. After ½ mile turn left off the roundabout by the Thames Valley Park Security building onto the drive towards David Lloyd fitness centre.

2. Pass to the left of the car park and around a metal field gate signposted 'Authorised vehicles only'. After ½ mile turn right alongside the river.

3. Follow the track by the river for 1 mile. The Lock Tea Gardens are just by Sonning Lock (no surprise!). For the Bull Inn, just before Sonning Bridge turn right and walk your bikes up past the church into the village.

West to Caversham Bridge
From the boat club turn left, with the Thames to your right. After ¼ mile, at the fork of rivers you have a choice:

(A) Bear left up over the bridge signposted 'Wallingford National Cycle Network Route 5' and follow this for 1½ miles as far as the second bridge with ornate balustrades and round lamp streetlights (Caversham Bridge).

(B) Stay on the path alongside the Kennet & Avon Canal and follow National Cycle Network Route 4 into the centre of Reading (or continue further west, joining Ride 2).

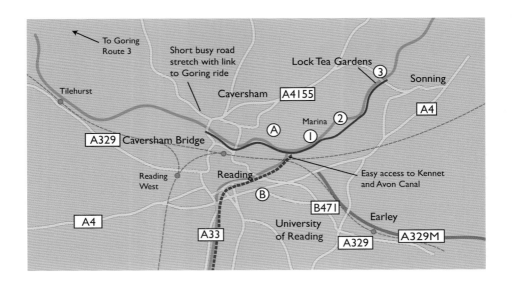

ROUTE 5
Forestry tracks from the Look Out, Bracknell

Distance: 5-mile circuit.

Map: Ordnance Survey Landranger map 175. Much more useful is the full colour leaflet called *Walks & Trails in Windsor Forest, Bracknell* which can be purchased at the Visitor Centre or from the adjacent Bike Hire outlet.

Website: www.bracknell-forest.gov.uk/lookout

Hills: There are several gentle hills.

Surface: Good-quality gravel tracks.

Roads and road crossings: None.

Refreshments: Cafe at the Visitor Centre.

Cycle Hire: Wellington Trek, at the Visitor Centre (07710 869 887) or go to www.wellingtontrek.co.uk

This area of the Crown Estate, Windsor comprises 2600 acres of predominantly Scots Pine woodland. The current policy is to increase the amount of broadleaf trees where appropriate. Although owned and managed by the Crown Estate Commissioners, the Look Out has been set up in partnership with the Bracknell Forest Borough Council. From the Look Out rides and tracks radiate through the forest. The ride suggested below is just one of many that could be devised along the wide gravel tracks that criss-cross the woodland. There is also a designated mountain bike area with tricky, testing single track should you be looking for something more challenging.

BACKGROUND AND PLACES OF INTEREST

The Discovery Outpost at the Look Out

Hands-on science fun with over 70 exhibits including 'Zones' covering Light and Colour, Sound and Communication, Forces and Movement, Woodland and Nature and Body and Perception. Open 10-5 daily.

Starting Point & Parking:

The Look Out is located in the woodland just to the south of Bracknell, about ¾ mile west of the roundabout at the junction of the B3430 and the A322 (Grid reference SU 878661).

ROUTE INSTRUCTIONS:

1. With your back to the entrance to the Look Out Visitor Centre go diagonally right towards Go Ape passing to the right of the coach park. Go through the gate.

2. Continue in the same direction on a broad track through pine trees. At the T-junction just before the tall Swinley Forest Post no. 1 turn sharp right signposted 'Pudding Hill'. After 600yds take the first left at a fork onto a similar broad stone track (no sign)

3. At a diagonal crossroads of tracks by Post no. 10 continue in the same direction uphill signposted 'MTB Trail' (red arrow) then very shortly at the next crossroads go straight ahead again, leaving the MTB trail which goes off to the left.

4. After almost 1 mile at Lower Star Post no. 5 (under power lines) continue straight ahead gently downhill.

5. At a fork bear right, keeping the Ministry of Defence wire fence to your left. Stay close to the fence around a sharp right-hand then left-hand bend. At the next flag, with 'Gate 8' to your left, by yellow and black 'H' (hydrant) signs, turn right.

6. Emerge at Upper Star Post no. 6 and take the second left signposted 'Caesar's Camp'. The latter can be explored on foot only.

7. At Post no. 8 turn right towards the Look Out, alongside a wood and wire fence. Good downhill. At the T-junction shortly after passing a pond on the right turn left.

8. Walk through the picnic area/cafe outdoor seating area to return to the car park.

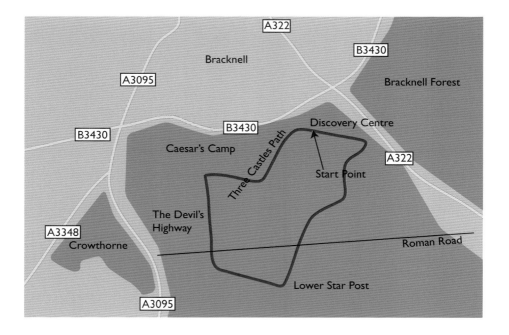

ROUTE 6
Windsor Great Park

Distance: 12-mile circuit.

Map: Ordnance Survey Landranger map 175. Maps of the Great Park are available from the Savill Garden Visitor Centre.

Website: www.theroyallandscape.co.uk

or www.thecrownestate.co.uk/windsor_great_park

Hills: There are several gentle hills.

Surface: All tarmac within Windsor Great Park. Stone-based tracks from the Windsor FC car park up to the park.

Roads and road crossings: The busy A332 at Ranger's Gate is crossed via a toucan crossing. The roads around Windsor Great Park carry very little estate traffic and it is travelling very slowly.

Cycling around the roads of Windsor Great Park is quite an extraordinary experience. There is only the absolute minimum of estate traffic, the landscaped parkland and magnificent trees are some of the finest you will ever see, there are superb views down Long Walk to Windsor Castle, a chance to see a polo match at Smith's Lawn or to combine your trip with a visit to the Savill Garden with its magnificent display of flowering shrubs and heathers. But perhaps most magical of all, especially for young children, are the big green gates around the deer enclosure that open with the push of a button. This remarkable oasis of tranquillity lies within just a few miles of the M3, M4, M25 and Heathrow. The park can be accessed from various car parks around its perimeter or there is a signed route from Windsor & Eton Football Club which is located on the southern edge of the town.

Starting Points & Parking:

There are several car parks around the perimeter of Windsor Great Park. The most convenient for this ride are:

1. Windsor – the car park by Windsor & Eton Football Club on the southern edge of Windsor, off the B3022 towards Winkfield. Just before the Stag & Hounds pub turn left by an off-licence onto St Leonards Road, signposted 'Windsor & Eton Football Club' (Grid reference SU 958755).

2. Ranger's Gate – there is a free car park just opposite Ranger's Gate on the A332 between Windsor and Ascot (Grid reference SU 953734).

ROUTE INSTRUCTIONS:

1. Exit the Windsor Football Club car park through a gate onto a cycle path. Shortly, at a 'Horse riders' sign, turn right. Climb gently.

2. Use the toucan crossing to cross the busy A332 into the park via Rangers Gate (alternative starting point). At a crossroads after ½ mile go straight ahead, signposted 'York Club'. Shortly at the next crossroads go straight ahead again (same sign).

3. Climb past York Club to a pink castle on a left-hand bend at the top. Descend, passing a statue of Queen Elizabeth on a horse to your right.

4. At the fork at the bottom of the hill bear right then go straight ahead at crossroads by a red-brick house (or turn right along Duke's Lane as far as Prince Consort's Gate to see the magnificent trees).

5. At the T-junction after passing the Royal School, at the top of a climb, turn right (*not* sharp right to Cumberland Lodge) then at the next T-junction turn right (again *not* Cumberland).

6. Continue straight ahead past Cumberland Gate Lodge then at the end of the polo ground turn left at a 'Guards Polo Club' sign.

7. At the next crossroads turn left: 'No entry for gardens traffic'. Go past the Savill Garden, following signs for 'Bishopgate' on a wide tarmac road, avoiding all 'No cycling' signs.

8. At the T-junction by Cumberland Gate turn right. Ignore left turns. Go past a large pink house, straight ahead at a crossroads then through big gates operated by a button.

9. Go past Long Walk (with views down towards Windsor Castle) and through a second set of gates. Ignore a left turn then at the crossroads shortly after passing Russel's Field Farm on the right, turn right signposted 'Rangers Gate exit' to rejoin the outward route.

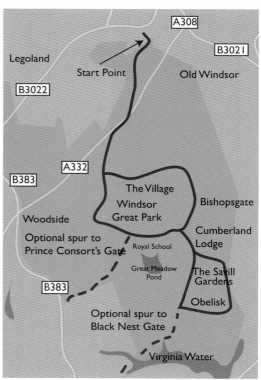

Legoland

Start Point

Old Windsor

A308

B3021

B3022

A332

B383

The Village
Windsor
Great Park

Bishopsgate

Woodside

Optional spur to
Prince Consort's Gate

Royal School

Great Meadow
Pond

Cumberland
Lodge

The Savill
Gardens

B383

Obelisk

Optional spur to
Black Nest Gate

Virginia Water

Distance: 4 miles one way, 8 miles return.

Map: Ordnance Survey Landranger map 175. Sustrans *Thames Valley Cycle Route* map shows various traffic-free options in the Windsor/Eton/Maidenhead area. Go to www.sustrans.org.uk

Hills: None.

Surface: Good stone-based tracks with some short rougher sections.

Roads and road crossings: A short section of quiet residential road takes you into the village of Bray from the end of the traffic-free section.

Refreshments: Crown pub, Hinds Head pub in Bray.

This short ride follows the Thames Valley west from the historic town of Windsor past Windsor race course to the pubs at the pretty village of Bray, using a mixture of cycle paths, riverside paths, tracks through newly planted woodlands and quiet residential roads. It goes right past the new rowing lake at Dorney created for Eton College. At the end of the lake you have the option of turning north to link to the trail alongside the Jubilee River, although until the planted woodland has grown to maturity this will be dominated by the noise of the nearby M4. The ride forms part of National Cycle Network Route 4 on its way from London to Reading and the West Country. By following the NCN 4 signs to the south you will go through Windsor to join Ride 6 around Windsor Great Park.

BACKGROUND AND PLACES OF INTEREST
Bray
Every street in this pretty village is lined with black and white cottages and houses. Legend has it that the local 16th-century vicar, Simon Aleyn, lived through four reigns and adjusted his religion to suit each monarch. Monkey Island, to the south of the village, has an 18th-century lodge decorated with unusual paintings of monkeys in costume.

Starting Point & Parking:
Windsor Leisure Centre (Grid reference SU 958772). There is a free car park along the route at Boveney, off the B3026 to the southeast of Dorney (Grid reference SU 937777).

ROUTE INSTRUCTIONS:

1. From the leisure centre go through the subway under the A332 then immediately turn right up the ramp. Cross the bridge over the Thames and bear left on a zigzag path down to the river.

2. Follow the stone then fine gravel path. This bears right away from the river then rejoins it. Easy to miss: keep an eye out for a right turn by a tall metal Millennium signpost on a wide tarmac path leading away from the river to continue on National Cycle Network Route 4.

3. Go through a gate then after 400 yards, on a right-hand bend, bear left onto a wide gravel track by a 'Footpath' and 'NCN Route 4' sign. At a wooden field gate about 50 yards before the Eton College Rowing Lake you have a choice of turning right on an off-road option on a grass/gravel track. If the road is not busy with rowing traffic you may prefer to use the road alongside the lake.

4. At the end of the lake and immediately after passing a small car park on your left, turn left, signposted 'Maidenhead 4' onto a narrow gravel path across the grass. The grass track turns to stone by the river. At the T-junction by the Millennium signpost turn right and cross the big wooden bridge over the river.

5. At the T-junction turn right 'NCN 4', join a residential road, and cross the motorway. At the T-junction in Bray with a black and white timbered house ahead, turn left signposted 'NCN Routes 4/52'. At the next T-junction by the memorial cross turn right (same sign). There are two pubs in Bray – the Crown and the Hinds Head.

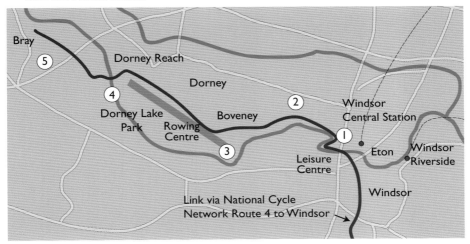

ROUTE 8
Grand Union Canal from Denham to Rickmansworth

Distance: 6 miles one way, 12 miles return.

Map: Ordnance Survey Landranger map 176.

Website: www.waterscape.com/canals-and-rivers/grand-union-canal

Hills: None.

Surface: Stone-based track with some rougher, bumpier sections. Mountain bikes or bikes with wide tyres are recommended.

Roads and road crossings: None.

Refreshments: Cafe at Denham Visitor Centre. Horse & Barge pub, South Harefield. Coy Carp pub, Coppermill Lane, Harefield. Cafe at the Aquadrome, Rickmansworth.

With the exception of a 5-mile section in London between Kensal Rise and Horsenden Hill (near Wembley), very little of the Grand Union Canal from Paddington right through to Uxbridge offers good recreational cycling: the towpath is too narrow, too rough, too overgrown or very slow with a succession of metal anti-motorbike barriers. To the north of Uxbridge things start to improve and Denham Country Park is a good starting point for exploration further north. Having said this, mountain bikes or bikes with wide tyres are definitely recommended as there are still some short rougher sections. The towpath is a green corridor past hundreds of brightly coloured narrowboats. The Batchworth Canal Visitor Centre or the cafe at the Aquadrome are good destinations although you have two options for extending your trip: along the Ebury Way (a railway path) into Watford, or on a continuation of the towpath to the west of Watford, towards Hemel Hempstead.

BACKGROUND AND PLACES OF INTEREST
Wildlife through the year
As the year progresses the dominant features of the ride change from birdsong in spring to wildflowers and dragonflies in the summer then berries on blackthorn, hawthorn and bramble in the autumn, offering important food sources for the resident thrushes and blackbirds but also migrants such as redwings and fieldfares.

Starting Points & Parking:
1. Denham Country Park – just north of the M40, Junction 1. Follow the brown and white signs from the roundabouts at the motorway junction (Grid reference TQ 047865).

2. Rickmansworth Aquadrome – it is a little complicated to describe how to get here! Take the A404 out of Rickmansworth towards Northwood and London. At the Moor Lane roundabout where 'A4145/Watford Road' is signposted straight on and 'London (A404)', off to the right, complete a circuit of the roundabout and head back towards Rickmansworth – the turning for the Aquadrome is on your left on Harefield Road (Grid reference TQ 057937).

ROUTE INSTRUCTIONS:

1. From the Denham Country Park Visitor Centre go back under the height barrier, turn left then right through the overflow car park, bearing left through the car park itself to pick up 'Grand Union Canal' signs. Follow the gravel path to the canal and turn left. Remember this point for your return (near Bridge 182).

2. Go past the tea gardens at the lock. About ½ mile after Bridge 180 and the Horse & Barge pub there is a rougher and narrower section to Bridge 179.

3. Go past the Coy Carp pub and Copper Mill Lock. The path is again a bit rougher either side of a concrete bridge with raised humps across it.

4. After 2 miles you will come to Batchworth Lock Visitor Centre, just beyond Rickmansworth Aquadrome. It is suggested you turn around here after visiting the centre and/or the cafe at the Aquadrome.

If you wish to extend your ride you can either stay on the Grand Union Canal towpath on its way towards Kings Langley and Hemel Hempstead or follow the Ebury Way along the course of an old railway line into Watford.

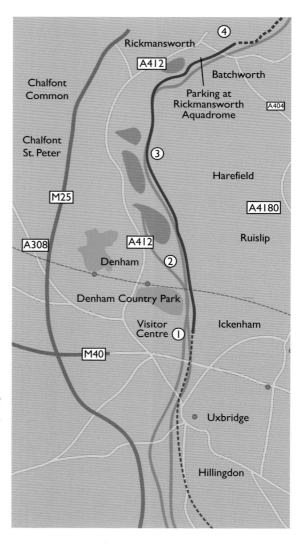

Distance: 5 miles one way, 10 miles return.

Map/leaflet: Ordnance Survey Landranger map 164. Also useful is the *Oxford Cycle Map*. See below for details.

Website: www.oxford.gov.uk > Council Services > Transport > Cycling
www.oxfordshire.gov.uk > Roads and transport > Cycling

Hills: None.

Surface: Good quality gravel tracks.

Roads and road crossings: Use the toucan crossing to cross St Aldates at Folly Bridge. Botley Road is crossed just west of the railway station via a toucan crossing.

Refreshments: Lots of choice in Oxford, most of it just off the route.
Isis Tavern by the Thames. Head of the River pub at Folly Bridge.
Waterman's Arms pub, East Street (south of the Botley Road).
Perch Inn, Binsey.

Oxford has always been a city dominated by bikes and recent developments have made cycling in the city more pleasant as the use of cars in the central area has been restricted still further. This ride explores the towpath of the Thames between the Ring Road at the south and the Perch pub at Binsey to the north. There are many architectural attractions along the way including the bridge at Iffley Lock and the folly at Folly Bridge. The southern half of this ride overlaps with National Cycle Network Route 5 which continues south via a cycle track alongside the railway to Radley and Abingdon.

NB This ride is also popular with walkers. Please ride with consideration for other users, let people know you are coming and thank them if they step aside for you. Where the path is narrow show courtesy by pulling in and letting walkers pass.

BACKGROUND AND PLACES OF INTEREST
Oxford
The centre of the city is dominated by the famous university with its scores of magnificent colleges and libraries. Children will particularly like the gargoyles along Queens Lane. When you have finished cycling perhaps you would like to try your hand at punting! Punts can be hired at Folly Bridge or Magdalen Bridge.

Starting Point and Parking:
Redbridge Park & Ride car park just off the Ring Road at the south of Oxford (at the junction of the A4144 and the A423, to the east of the A34).

Alternatively if starting from central Oxford the Thames towpath can be joined at Folly Bridge or just west of the railway station on Botley Road.

ROUTE INSTRUCTIONS:

1. Exit Redbridge Park & Ride car park via the entrance and turn right along the cycle path (away from Oxford). Descend through the subway and at the first T-junction turn left to go through a second subway. At the second T-junction (with metal barriers to your left) turn right and follow the cycle track parallel with the Ring Road.

2. Cross a bridge over a tributary of the Thames then just before the much larger bridge over the main course of the Thames turn left downhill signposted 'National Cycle Network Route 5' then left along the towpath. (Remember this point for your return).

3. Go past the lock, the Isis Tavern and past the college boathouses. At the crossroads by Folly Bridge use the toucan crossing to go straight ahead onto a continuation of the towpath.

4. Walk your bike through Osney Lock. Descend off the towpath onto East Street by the Waterman's Arms pub and continue in the same direction parallel with the river. As the street swings round to the left climb the steps up to the Botley Road.

5. Cross to the other side of the road to join a continuation of the towpath (now on the right side of the river). You may prefer to cross the road using the toucan crossings that lie to the east or west of the bridge.

6. Cross a hump-backed metal and wooden bridge and turn left following the Thames Path. Follow this with water to both left and right. After ½ mile go straight ahead past the marina and turn left on the bridge across the river.

7. Go past the boatyard then follow the main wide stone track as it swings left away from the river to arrive at the Perch pub.

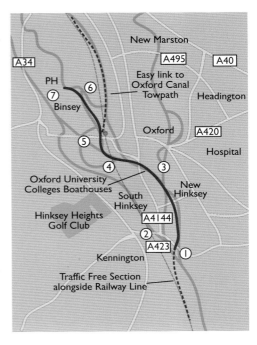

ROUTE 10
Phoenix Trail

Distance: 7 miles one way, 14 miles return.

Map: Ordnance Survey Landranger map 165.

Website: www.sustrans.org.uk or www.chilternsaonb.org

Hills: None.

Surface: Good stone-based track or tarmac.

Roads and road crossings: The one busy road crossed in Thame is via a toucan crossing. If you visit or start from Princes Risborough you will need to use roads between the bridge over the railway at the end of Horsenden Lane and the centre of town.

Refreshments: Lots of choice in Thame and Princes Risborough. Towersey Arms pub in Towersey, about 2 miles east of Thame.

A section of the old railway line that used to link Princes Risborough to Oxford has been converted to recreational use and offers a fine open ride across the Oxfordshire countryside with wide-ranging views to the steep wooded escarpment of the Chiltern Hills which lie to the south. Red Kites have been introduced to this area and you will see many of these majestic birds with their distinctive forked tails as they wheel high above. Some more unusual animals can also be seen along the trail: about halfway along, perched high up on poles are a set of bizarre metal animal sculptures. This is one of those good 'conversational' rides where the path is wide, with a fine smooth surface allowing you to cycle side by side and set the world to rights. This is best done on a weekday or out of season as the ride is very popular on summer weekends, as is the Towersey Arms, the only pub along the route.

Starting Point & Parking:

Thame Leisure/Sports Centre, on the west side of Thame, about 300 yards east of the roundabout at the junction of the A418 and A329 (Grid reference SP 696058).

NB There is no parking along Horsenden Lane at the eastern end of the Phoenix Trail. There is space for a few cars just off the B4009 immediately south of the old green metal railway bridge between Princes Risborough and Chinnor (Grid reference SP 786036).

ROUTE INSTRUCTIONS:

1. From the Thame Leisure Centre car park aim to pass between the white buildings of the leisure centre and the school. Go straight ahead at a mini-roundabout, then first left, keeping the leisure centre buildings close by on your right. Follow a tarmac path across the playing field to join the Phoenix Trail. Turn right. (Remember this point for the return trip).

2. Follow the trail as it swings left (east). Go straight ahead at a crossroads of tracks signposted 'Towersey 2, Princes Risborough 7, National Cycle Network Route 57'.

3. Use the toucan crossing to cross the busy road by the industrial estate.

4. Go past a wooden 'Clam' sculpture. The Towersey Arms pub is shortly after this on your left.

5. Go past animal sculptures on the top of tall poles.

6. The railway path itself finishes 2 miles after passing the animals, at the bridge over the busy B4009. You may wish to turn around here if you do not want to go into Princes Risborough.

7. (On to Princes Risborough). There is a short rough section then at the T-junction with tarmac by Glebe Cottage turn right (remember this point for the return trip).

8. Go past the church. At the T-junction at the end of Horsenden Lane turn left over the railway bridge and immediately left again following the National Cycle Network Route 57 signs into the centre of Princes Risborough. This will involve busier roads.

Exit from Princes Risborough

The waymarked Route 57 provides an alternative to the A4010/B4444 from the centre of Princes Risborough to the start of the Phoenix Trail. The route is as follows: Market Square, Church Street, Stratton Road, Manor Park Avenue, Station Road, Picts Lane, Horsenden Lane.

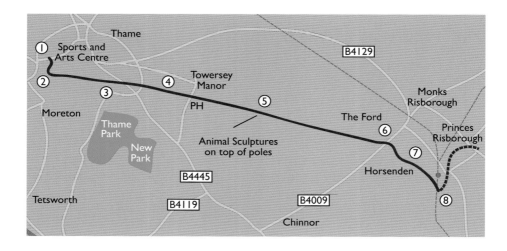

ROUTE 11
Wendover Woods, southeast of Aylesbury

Distance: 6 mile-circuit with several opportunities for short cuts.

Map/leaflet: Ordnance Survey Landranger map 165. The Forestry Commission produce an A4 full colour leaflet called *Wendover Woods – In the Chiltern Hills*. Go to www.forestry.gov.uk and type 'Wendover Woods' into the 'Search' box.

Hills: Lots of hills! The car park is at the top of the hill so every ride starts with a descent and finishes with a climb.

Surface: Stone and gravel forestry tracks.

Roads and road crossings: None.

Refreshments: Excellent cafe at the start.

There are very few Forestry Commission holdings of any size in the area immediately to the north and west of London. Wendover Woods are the one exception and are the only woodland in the area with waymarked trails aimed at recreational family cycling. There are some wonderful views and the car park at the start of the ride is very close to the highest point of the Chilterns. The woodland is mainly broadleaf so there is a fantastic display of bluebells in the late spring and a glorious riot of colour in the autumn as the trees start to lose their leaves. The only downside to this otherwise perfect combination is that with the car park/starting point at the top of the hill almost all the routes start off with a descent and finish with a climb back up to the car park. You have been warned!

NB There are also plenty of testing mountain bike trails in the nearby Aston Hill Woods. There is a Forestry Commission policy of trying to keep family cyclists and experienced mountain bikers apart so if you are super fit and feel you have not been tested by the routes in Wendover Woods, why not try Aston Hill Woods? You will need to buy a day permit to use Aston Hill Woods which gives you third party insurance. Go to www.forestry.gov.uk or www.rideastonhill.co.uk for further details.

BACKGROUND AND PLACES OF INTEREST
Wendover Woods
These woods were originally owned by the Rothschild family and were transferred to the Forestry Commission in 1939. During the Rothschild era the wood was used extensively by the family and their guests for recreational purposes - mainly shooting and horse riding. It is reported that Lord Rothschild would be driven into the woods by a team of zebras to picnic at one of his favourite spots, now known locally as 'Rothschild's Seat'.

Starting Point & Parking:
From Wendover follow the A4011 north towards Tring. After 3 miles take the first proper road to the right towards Buckland Common and Cholesbury. The entrance to the woodland is ¾ mile up this steep minor road on the right hand side. Climb on the road through the forest for about 1 mile to the car parks/cafe at the top of the hill.

ROUTE INSTRUCTIONS:

1. From the Wendover Woods car park continue past the cafe on the tarmac road towards the exit. After 200 yards keep an eye out for a turning to the right by a tall wooden post with a purple arrow (Firecrest Trail). This is the start of the Family Cycle Route.

2. Gentle descent with great views to the right. After ⅔ mile at a major track junction where the purple trail turns sharp right, either continue straight ahead for the main route or turn right for the short cut route, avoiding one big hill.

3. After a further ⅔ mile, at a track crossroads, turn right (signs will tell you where you can't go) to continue downhill. At a second crossroads, with a wide stone forestry road at the bottom of a much steeper section, turn right uphill climbing steadily or steeply.

4. At a T-junction with 'Short Cut' signposted to the right, turn left for the main route (or right for the short cut). At the next major track junction turn right uphill then shortly at another T-junction turn left for the main route or right for a short cut.

5. The track surface becomes rougher. After ⅓ mile, at a fork on the descent bear right. At a T-junction by wooden benches bear left. After a further ⅓ mile, immediately after a wooden barrier by a turning circle with a grass 'roundabout' bear left past wooden fitness equipment for the full route (or go straight ahead for short cut).

6. Gentle descent. At a fork bear right on the upper track. At a T-junction turn right sharply back on yourself uphill to return to the start.

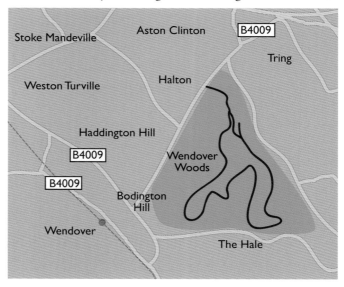

ROUTE 12
Grand Union Canal from Apsley Marina, Hemel Hempstead to Tring Reservoir

Distance: 12 miles one way, 24 miles return.

Map: Ordnance Survey Landranger maps 165 and 166.

Website: www.waterscape.com/canals-and-rivers/grand-union-canal

Hills: None.

Surface: Mainly a good stone or fine gravel path but there are some short, rougher, more overgrown sections between Cow Roast and Bulbourne.

Roads and road crossings: No dangerous crossings.

Refreshments: Red Lion pub, Woody's Vegetarian Restaurant, Hemel Hempstead. Fishery Inn, Boxmoor. Three Horseshoes pub, Bourne End. Lots of choice in Berkhamsted. Grand Junction Arms pub, Bulbourne. Bluebell Cafe, White Lion pub, Anglers Retreat pub, Marsworth.

The Grand Union Canal connects London to Birmingham but it would be a brave person to jump on their bike at one end and imagine a straightforward ride to the other. There is an enormous variety of surfaces you will encounter from very rough and rutted to fine, smooth gravel. Parts may be overgrown with vegetation, other parts are very narrow and then there are barriers to keep out motorbikes. So it is best to pick and choose the best bits, and parts of this ride, through Berkhamsted, for example, are as good as it gets. However, even on a ride like this there are short rougher sections, so be prepared for these. The ride runs alongside Tring Summit, the highpoint of the canal between London and the Midlands; to the north it drops down to Milton Keynes and to the south towards London. You won't be stuck for refreshments on this ride as there are cafes at both ends and many pubs along the way, especially through Berkhamsted.

BACKGROUND AND PLACES OF INTEREST

Tring

The River Bulbourne is a chalk stream which rises near Cow Roast and flows for 7 miles to join the River Gade in Hemel Hempstead. It originally flowed through cattle-grazed meadows hence the name Bulbourne or 'river of the bulls'. At two points the river disappears as it merges with the canal. Since 1797 the Bulbourne has been the main source of water for the Grand Union Canal.

Tring Cutting

30ft deep and 1½ miles long, the Tring Cutting was a major feat of engineering completed in 1797. It was another two years before the Tring Summit was connected to the canal at Berkhamsted as the sandy Hertfordshire soil meant that bricks had to be ferried from London.

Cow Roast Lock

Its name derives from 'Cow Rest' as this area was the location of large cattle pens used by drovers on route to London from the Midlands. The lock is the first descending south from the Midlands.

Starting Points & Parking:

1. Tring Reservoirs – Startops (reservoir) car park, north of Tring, on the B489 in Marsworth just southwest of the White Lion pub (Grid reference SP 920140).
2. Apsley Marina/Nash Mills, Hemel Hempstead – just off the A4251 to the east of Apsley railway station (Grid reference TL 064050).

ROUTE INSTRUCTIONS:

1. From the Old Red Lion pub (Nash Mills, at the southern edge of Hemel Hempstead) follow the canal towpath northwest towards Berkhamsted. Go past Apsley Marina.

2. Go past the Fishery Inn then after 1 mile, another marina and the Three Horseshoes pub.

3. The path improves through Berkhamsted as you pass several pubs and information boards about the history of the canal and the town itself.

4. The surface is good as far as Cow Roast Lock. After this the path becomes narrower and at times overgrown. This is the summit section of the canal.

5. The towpath improves again at Bulbourne as the canal starts its descent. It is suggested you go as far as Marsworth where there is a cafe and two pubs. There is also a car park here where you may prefer to start.

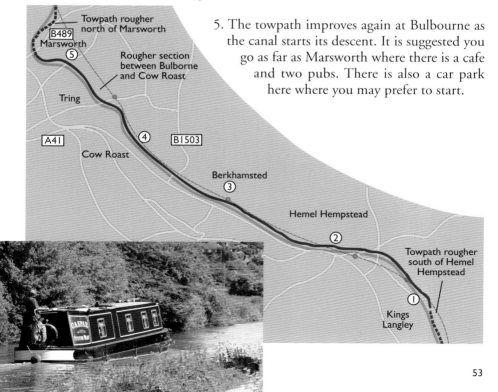

ROUTE 13

A circuit in Ashridge Estate, north of Berkhamsted

Tring Station 1
Tring 2¾

Valiant Trooper
Public House

Berkhamsted **4**
LT Gaddesden 3½

Recreation Ground
Parking

Distance: 4 ½-mile circuit plus a 2-mile spur north from the monument towards Ivinghoe Beacon.

Map: Ordnance Survey Landranger map 165. A free cycle map is available from the Visitor Centre or available as a download (see below).

Website: The main site for Ashridge Estate can be found on www.nationaltrust.org.uk or you can download a free map of the cycle routes at:
www.nationaltrust.org.uk/main/w-cycle_routes_at_ashridge.pdf
www.chilternsaonb.org/site_details.asp?siteID=20

Hills: There is one major hill, to return to the start.

Surface: Mixed quality. Some good gravel tracks and some rougher sections which will be muddy in winter or after prolonged rain. Mountain bikes are recommended.

Roads and road crossings: Care should be taken on the two crossings of the B4506. A ½ mile section of the minor road to Aldbury is used on the return part of the ride.

Refreshments: There is a good cafe next to the Visitor Centre. Otherwise the nearest refreshments are either in the village of Aldbury or in Berkhamsted.

Comprising over 1600 hectares of woodlands, commons, downland and farmland, the Ashridge Estate runs along the main ridge of the Chilterns from Berkhamsted to Ivinghoe Beacon. The main focal point of the Estate is the granite monument erected in 1832 in honour of the 3rd Duke of Bridgewater, father of inland navigation, who was nicknamed 'the Canal Duke'. The ride starts from this mighty monument (which you can climb!) and descends through broadleaf woodland on a series of bridleways marked with blue arrows. This is just one of many rides that could be devised in the estate. Be warned, however, that these are woodland tracks rather than specially built cycle trails so the going can become muddy in winter and after prolonged rain. Mountain bikes are recommended.

Starting Point & Parking:

The Ashridge Estate car park by the Visitor Centre. From the A41/Berkhamsted follow the B4506 north for 3½ miles towards Ringshall and Dunstable taking the second road to the left to the Visitor Centre.

ROUTE INSTRUCTIONS:

1. With your back to the cafe and facing the Bridgewater monument turn left on a broad tarmac path which soon becomes a wide track signposted with a blue arrow: 'Bridleway'.

2. Ignore a first left signposted 'No horses, no bikes'. After 300 yards of steep descent, at an obvious fork of tracks, bear left on the upper track. At a track T-junction by a telephone pole turn left uphill.

3. Shortly go straight ahead past a house with a high surrounding hedge on your left. Continue in the same direction.

4. Long gentle descent. At the B4506 go straight ahead (take care) onto the track opposite signposted 'Berkhamsted Common'. Continue descending on slightly rougher track.

5. At a fork after ½ mile bear right then at the crossroads shortly after passing a house to the left, turn right uphill on a broad stone 'drive' (blue arrow).

WELCOME
to the Ashridge Estate
Visitor Centre

Tea Room
Gift Shop
Toilets

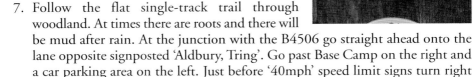

6. At the next crossroads of tracks (with a red-brick barn 50 yards ahead) turn right on a broad stone track (blue arrow). Shortly, at a 'Little Coldharbour Farm' sign, bear right away from the stone track onto a narrower track (blue arrow) and soon fork right again.

7. Follow the flat single-track trail through woodland. At times there are roots and there will be mud after rain. At the junction with the B4506 go straight ahead onto the lane opposite signposted 'Aldbury, Tring'. Go past Base Camp on the right and a car parking area on the left. Just before '40mph' speed limit signs turn right onto a track signposted 'Bridgewater Monument'.

8. After 200 yards at a crossroads of tracks turn right then at the house with its high surrounding edge, turn left to rejoin the outward route, soon forking right. After a gentle descent, the last ¼ mile back to the monument is steep and you may prefer to push.

Duncombe Terrace Route
There is also a 2-mile there-and-back ride on a broad stone track that heads due north from the Bridgewater monument through magnificent beechwood woodland as far as the Ivinghoe Beacon road, offering fine views west towards Wendover Woods.

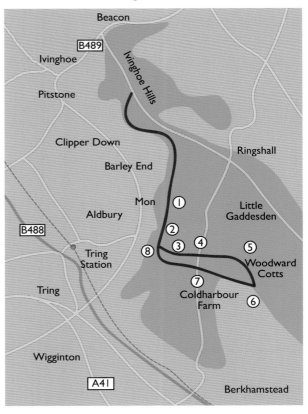

ROUTE 14

Nickey Line, between Harpenden and Hemel Hempstead

Distance: 6 miles one way, 12 miles return.

Map: Ordnance Survey Landranger map 166.

Website: www.nickeyline.org or www.welhat.gov.uk

Hills: Steady climb from Harpenden towards Redbourn.

Surface: Good stone-based tracks, tarmac.

Roads and road crossings: Three busy roads are crossed – two at the roundabout of the B487 with the A5183 near Redbourn and a second crossing of the B487 close to the M1. Each of these roads may be busy and great care should be taken if you are with young children. If you continue into the centre of Hemel Hempstead you will need to use roads.

Refreshments: None on the route itself. Plenty of choice in Harpenden or Hemel Hempstead.

The reasons for the railway being called the Nickey Line are a matter of dispute: some say that it derives from the half-length trousers called knickerbockers either because these were worn by the navvies building the line or because the line was considered half-size being only single track. The name may also have come from 'funicular' referring to the exceptionally steep gradients. It may even come from the church of St Nicholas in Harpenden. From Harpenden the ride climbs then descends through lush countryside, the verges ablaze with colour from the profusion of wildflowers in spring and summer. There are three roads to cross where great care should be exercised as they can be busy. Pass through the long tunnel under the widened M1 to finish on the northern edge of Hemel Hempstead.

BACKGROUND AND PLACES OF INTEREST
The Nickey Line
The London to Birmingham Railway line was completed in 1838 and a branch line was proposed by the businessmen of Hemel Hempstead to link the straw plait trade in the town with the hat-makers of Luton. Thus the Nickey Line was born and opened in 1877. It carried passengers until 1947 and freight until 1979.

Starting Point & Parking:
Park Hill, Harpenden. Take the A1081 Luton Road out of Harpenden and immediately after passing under a railway bridge turn sharp left onto Park Hill. Park towards the top of the hill on the left, near to a gap in the trees to the left giving access to the railway path (Grid reference TL 126149).

ROUTE INSTRUCTIONS:

1. Park at the top of Park Hill to avoid most of the climb but remember where you join the path for your return or you risk flying past your exit from the trail and being faced with a steep climb back up the hill.

2. Climb gently then descend. At the roundabout after 1½ miles, cross the B487 and A5183 with great care following National Cycle Network Route 57 signs.

3. After ¾ mile at the fork bear left to avoid steps. At the road turn right then left.

4. After a further ¾ mile re-cross the B487 then shortly after go through the tunnel under the M1.

5. After 2 miles the trail ends abruptly opposite Euro Car Parts on Eastman Trading Estate on the edge of Hemel Hempstead. It is suggested you turn around at this point to return.

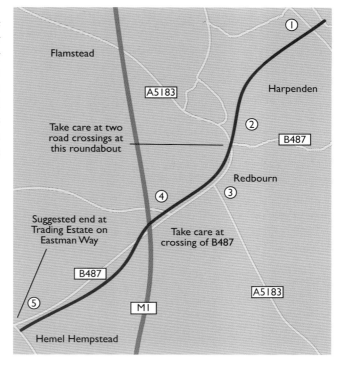

Flamstead

A5183

Harpenden

Take care at two road crossings at this roundabout

B487

Redbourn

Suggested end at Trading Estate on Eastman Way

Take care at crossing of B487

B487

A5183

M1

Hemel Hempstead

ROUTE 15
Alban Way from Hatfield to St. Albans

Distance: 6 miles one way, 12 miles return.

Map: Ordnance Survey Landranger map 166. See also websites below for downloadable maps.

Website: www.hertsdirect.org, www.stacc.org.uk www.welhat.gov.uk

Hills: None.

Surface: Good stone-based tracks, tarmac.

Roads and road crossings: There are several road crossings and short sections of residential roads are used at several points along the trail.

Refreshments: None on the route, lots of choice in St Albans or Hatfield.

A popular railway path between Hatfield and St Albans where you have the impression of passing along a green wooded corridor despite the fact that much of the route is within the urban area of the two towns. For the shopaholics in the group there is the chance to get your fix at the Galleria Shopping Mall right by the A1. As you approach St Albans there are fine views across to the cathedral. This is one of several railway paths in Hertfordshire, the others being the Nickey Line, the Ayot Greenway and the Cole Green Way, all covered elsewhere in the book.

BACKGROUND AND PLACES OF INTEREST
The old railway
Opened in 1865 by the Hatfield & St Albans Railway Company, it was absorbed by the Great Northern Railway in 1883. Passenger services continued to 1951 and freight trains ran until the late 1960s. In 1985 the line was given a new lease of life when it was converted to recreational use.

St Albans
All that is left of Verulamium, once the most important Roman town in Britain, lies to the west of the present city of St Albans. There are remains of the great amphitheatre and part of an underground heating system. The Verulamium Museum contains some spectacular mosaic pavements. Modern St Albans takes its name from Alban, the first Christian martyr in Britain.

Starting Points & Parking:
1. Hatfield: from A1(M) Junction 4 take the A414 towards Hertford then after ¼ mile turn right at the roundabout onto Great North Road. As this swings right and becomes Longmead bear left by a car dealership onto a continuation of Great North Road. Park at the top, beyond the Wrestlers pub and just before the 'No through road' sign. The cycle path starts on your right just before the bridge (Grid reference TL 232094).

2. St Albans: start from the crossroads of Leyland Avenue, Mentmore Road and Cottonmill Lane, just to the east of Abbey Station. (Take Prospect Road from the A5183 near the station). After parking (no specific car park) take the track leading past Sopwell Youth Club, then turn left under the railway arch (Grid reference TL 150061).

ROUTE INSTRUCTIONS:

1. From the top of Great North Road turn right onto the cycle path just before the bridge over the railway. After ¾ mile at a fork bear right to cross the road by Fiddlebridge Industrial Centre. At the road junction turn right then left opposite De Havilland Close.

2. Pass under the subway following National Cycle Network Route 61 signs. Turn right to cross the bridge over the A1 then left opposite Galleria shopping mall to continue along the Alban Way.

3. Move from town into the countryside, passing a small lake to your left.

4. Cross a road beyond a metal barrier, pass through a residential area and go past Body Limits Gymnasium.

5. After 1 mile pass under an enormous brick arch. After a further ½ mile at a T-junction just beyond a red-brick and concrete bridge turn right signposted 'Abbey Station, City Centre, Harpenden'. The traffic-free trail shortly ends.

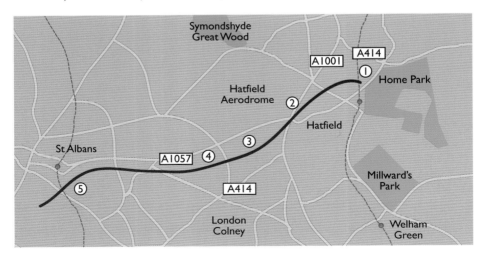

ROUTE 16
Ayot Greenway, east from Wheathampstead

Distance: 3½ miles one way, 7 miles return.

Map: Ordnance Survey Landranger map 166. See also websites below for downloadable maps.

Website: www.hertsdirect.org www.stacc.org.uk www.welhat.gov.uk

Hills: Gentle climb from west to east.

Surface: Good stone-based tracks, tarmac.

Roads and road crossings: Short section on road in Wheathampstead to get to the start of the trail.

Refreshments: Lots of choice in Wheathampstead.

A short ride along the course of the old Luton, Dunstable and Welwyn Junction Railway with a long gentle climb through beautiful mature broadleaf woodland. The only obvious way of extending the ride is on the network of quiet undulating lanes at the eastern end of the ride, perhaps visiting George Bernard Shaw's home in Ayot St Lawrence.

BACKGROUND AND PLACES OF INTEREST
History of Wheathampstead
According to the Domesday book there were once four mills on the River Lea at Wheathampstead. The present mill is a 17th century timber-framed building. The mill leat was created to provide a head of water to turn the mill wheel for grinding wheat into flour. Many of the village's historic buildings are close to the river. St Helens Parish Church, originally of Saxon origin, was rebuilt and embellished during the period 1230-1330. The Bull Inn dates from the 16th century and Izaak Walton, author of *The Compleat Angler*, is said to have been a guest here.

Starting Point & Parking:
Wheathampstead. Free car park near the Bull pub. NB it is the car park beyond the Bull's own car park (Grid reference TL 178142).

ROUTE INSTRUCTIONS:
1. From the free car park return to the High Street by the Bull pub. Turn right to cross the bridge over the river then after 50 yards turn right onto Mount Road, following signs for 'Ayot Greenway, Welwyn Garden City, National Cycle Network Routes 12/57'.

2. Fine wide smooth gravel track. Pass through several bridle gates. At the T-junction turn left 'Ayot Greenway' (remember this spot for the return leg).

3. Gentle climb. At a crossroads of tracks turn right, signposted 'Ayot Greenway'.

4. Lovely gentle climb through mature broadleaf woodland. The traffic-free section ends at its junction with Ayot St Peter Road.

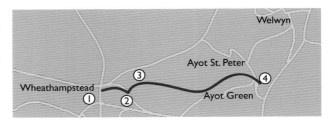

ROUTE 17
Milton Keynes to Winslow along National Cycle Network Route 51

Distance: 9 miles one way, 18 miles return.

Map: Ordnance Survey Landranger maps 165 and 152. Better is the Milton Keynes Redway map (see website below).

Website: www.mkweb.co.uk/cycling/home.asp

Hills: Several gentle climbs.

Surface: Good stone-based tracks, tarmac.

Roads and road crossings: Take care at the crossing of Buckingham Road (B4034) on the southwestern edge of Milton Keynes. Several sections of quiet roads are used. There is a little more traffic if you go right into the centre of Winslow.

Refreshments: Lots of choice in Milton Keynes and Winslow.

This 9-mile section of the National Cycle Network connects the astonishing urban cycle network of Milton Keynes Redway to the small attractive old town of Winslow via cycle paths and quiet lanes across the gently undulating Buckinghamshire countryside. The ride starts from near the National Bowl at the distinctive silver star sculpture on the eastern edge of Furzton Lake and follows the cycle path that runs along Emerson Valley almost to the edge of town. A succession of Rights of Way have been improved with stone and gravel to create a route that travels almost due southwest to the edge of Winslow with its handsome red-brick buildings and fine square. There are plenty of refreshments available at several cafes and pubs.

BACKGROUND AND PLACES OF INTEREST
Winslow Hall
One of the finest buildings in Buckinghamshire, Winslow Hall is thought to have been designed by Sir Christopher Wren in about 1700, some 25 years after he designed St Paul's Cathedral in London. It was built for William Lowndes, a local boy who made his fortune in London and rose to be Secretary of the Treasury.

Starting Points & Parking:
1. Furzton Lake, just off the A421 on the south-western edge of Milton Keynes (Grid reference SP 851359).
2. Winslow, on the A413 Buckingham – Aylesbury road to the southwest of Milton Keynes (Grid reference SP 771279).

ROUTE INSTRUCTIONS:
1. Follow the cycle path around the east side of Furzton Lake towards a tall silver star metal sculpture, soon picking up signs for 'National Cycle Network Route 51, Winslow'.

2. Turn left after passing a cricket pavilion on the left, following the path around the cricket pitch/playing field to your left. Shortly after crossing a small stream turn right (all NCN 51 signs).

3. Follow the route along the valley for just over 1 mile. Immediately after passing under the second large concrete bridge turn sharp left uphill by a tall metal Millennium signpost. Follow the cycle path alongside V2 (Tattenhoe Street) under the subway then right alongside H8 (Standing Way).

4. Follow NCN 51 round to the left alongside Buckingham Road then after ¼ mile take care turning right onto the track (NCN 51) on the other side of the road.

5. Continue in the same direction at several crossroads over the next 3½ miles. The trail briefly joins the lane network following signs for Swanbourne, then on a sharp left-hand bend after ⅔ mile bear right onto a no through road by a 'Moco Farm' sign. Shortly as the farm road swings right bear left through a gate onto a track.

6. The track turns to tarmac. At a T-junction with a wider road turn right on the shared-use pavement then shortly right again.

7. The route into Winslow town centre uses several roads and cycle paths but is well signposted. There are plenty of pubs, cafes and tearooms.

ROUTE 18
Grand Union Canal from Bletchley to Leighton Buzzard

Distance: 7½ miles one way, 15 miles return.

Map: Ordnance Survey Landranger maps 152 and 165. Better is the map produced by Sustrans.

Website: www.sustrans.org.uk

Hills: None.

Surface: Good stone-based track.

Roads and road crossings: No dangerous crossings.

Refreshments: Lots of choice in Bletchley/Water Eaton.
Grand Union pub, Three Locks. Globe Inn, just north of Leighton Buzzard.
Lots of choice in Leighton Buzzard. Grove Lock pub, south of the A505.

The Grand Union Canal near Milton Keynes is featured twice in this guide: Ride 21 explores the canal north from the centre of the town along the Broadwalk as far as Cosgrove to the northwest; this ride heads due south from the southern edge of town to Leighton Buzzard. The towpath on the middle section between these two rides has a much poorer surface. By contrast, the recent improvements to the towpath south of Bletchley mean this is one of the best stretches for cycling on the whole canal between London to Birmingham. The excellent quality continues south beyond the centre of Leighton Buzzard for another 1½ miles to the pub near Grove Lock then abruptly turns to grass.

BACKGROUND AND PLACES OF INTEREST
Bletchley Park
During the World War 2, codebreakers at Bletchley Park decrypted messages from a large number of Axis powers, most importantly the ciphers generated by the German Enigma machines. Bletchley Park is now a museum displaying one of the famous Enigma machines.

Starting Points & Parking:
1. Bletchley/Water Eaton – follow the A4146 south from the A5 towards Leighton Buzzard. At the first roundabout go straight ahead (Great Brickhill is to the left); at the second roundabout turn right and almost immediately, at the third roundabout (Lomond Road/Stoke Road) turn right into the small car park next to the canal (Grid reference SP 884318).

2. Leighton Buzzard – the canal runs right past Tesco in the centre of town. The nearest car park is just west of the canal, off Old Road at the junction of Wing Road and New Road (Grid reference SP 915240).

ROUTE INSTRUCTIONS:

1. From the A4146 car park by Bridge 99 in Bletchley/Water Eaton follow the towpath south with the canal to your right.

2. After 2½ miles go past the Grand Union pub at Three Locks.

3. After another 2½ miles follow NCN 6 signs past the Globe Inn and Wyvern Shipping Boat Hire just north of Leighton Buzzard town centre.

4. The good-quality towpath continues beyond Leighton Buzzard for a further 1½ miles as far as the Grove Lock pub.

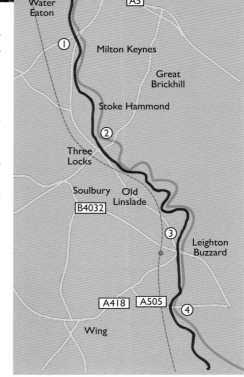

Distance: 12 miles – approximately 3 miles for the circuit of Willen Lakes, 3 miles for the circuit of Caldecotte Lake and 3 miles each way for the linking section along the Ouzel River.

Map/leaflet: Ordnance Survey Landranger map 152. Far more useful is the Milton Keynes Redway Map, showing the vast network of cycle lanes in the area (see website below).

Website: Website: www.mkweb.co.uk/cycling is an excellent website with plenty of interest for every sort of cyclist. You can also download the Redway map for free. See also: www.mkparks.co.uk

Hills: There are no hills.

Surface: Excellent quality tracks.

Roads and road crossings: There is only one road crossing, at the southern end of the ride and this is not a busy road.

Refreshments: Cafe at the Willen Water sports centre. Lakeside pub, Willen South Lake. Caldecotte Arms pub on Caldecotte Lake.

Milton Keynes has a tremendous amount to offer by way of safe, attractive family cycling. This ride runs along the valley formed by the River Ouzel, linking Willen Lake and Caldecotte Lake, the two largest expanses of water in Milton Keynes. Willen Lake is also a major centre for water sports so you will probably see many brightly coloured sails of windsurfers and dinghies on the water. Near to Willen Lake is a Buddhist Pagoda and a maze which are both well worth a visit. The ride takes you past woodland and along the willow trees lining the banks of the river. As you approach Caldecotte Lake you will see the windmill which stands on its shores. A complete circuit of the lake, with the chance of refreshment at the Caldecotte Arms pub, points you back in the right direction for your return along the river back to the start at Willen Lake.

Starting Point & Parking:

The car park on the western shore of Willen Lakes. Follow signs west from M1 Junction 14 or follow the A509 (H5) east from the A5 towards the M1. There are plenty of signs for Willen Lakes (Grid reference SP 873405).

ROUTE INSTRUCTIONS:

1. From the Willen Lake car park go to the path at the water's edge and turn right. Follow the lakeside path around the edge of the lake (with the water to your left), going past the Aerial Adventure playground.

2. At the T-junction where the main track continues around the edge of the lake, turn right following signs for 'Milton Keynes Village and the Ouzel Valley'. For the next 3 miles you are following signs for 'Riverside Walk, Walton Lake and Caldecotte'.

3. Keep the river on your left, do not cross bridges over it for 3 miles. At the T-junction with the road (Simpson Road) turn left then right through the metal height barrier bearing diagonally right through the car park to pick up signs for 'Caldecotte Lake'.

4. Complete a circuit of the lake – head towards the windmill, keeping the water on your left. Go past the Caldecotte Arms pub and the birdwatching point. Stay on the paths closest to the water's edge. At times this is a bit confusing, but you'll soon find the right path!

5. On the return follow signs for 'Simpson' and 'Riverside Walk'. At the dam at the northern end of the lake bear right, away from the water, to join a wide cycle path alongside the road.

6. Rejoin the outward route near the Simpson Road car park (mentioned in Instruction 3), cross the river on the road bridge then turn right to re-enter Ouzel Valley Park, following signs for 'Walton Lake and Woughton on the Green'.

7. Keep the river to the right (do not cross it) and stay on the broad tarmac path, following signs for 'Riverside Walk, Woughton on the Green, Woolstones'. Continue in the same direction to join the lakeside path alongside Willen Lake, keeping the water to your left.

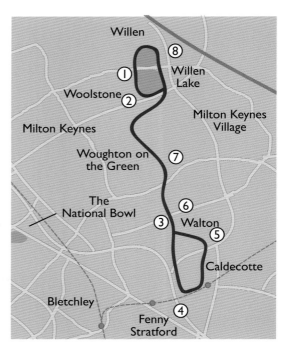

8. Follow signs for 'Willen Lakes North' and 'Willen Village'. At the north end of the North Lake follow the shoreline round to the left past the Peace Pagoda to return to the start.

ROUTE 20
Along the River Great Ouse through Milton Keynes

Distance: 7 miles one way, 14 miles return.

Map/leaflet: Ordnance Survey Landranger map 152. Far more useful is the Milton Keynes Redway Map, showing the vast network of cycle lanes in the area (see below for details).

Website: www.mkweb.co.uk/cycling is an excellent website with plenty of interest for every sort of cyclist. You can also download the Redway map for free.

Hills: There are no hills.

Surface: Excellent quality tracks, mainly sealed surface.

Roads and road crossings: The one road crossing where extra care should be taken is right at the start of the ride, near Old Stratford. At the eastern end of the ride, you will need to use roads if you wish to go into the centre of Newport Pagnell.

Refreshments: Lots of choice in Old Stratford at the start of the ride. Pubs just off the route where the railway path crosses the Grand Union Canal (both north and south along the towpath). Lots of choice in Newport Pagnell.

For those who have not yet discovered the secret: Milton Keynes offers more miles of safe and enjoyable family cycling than any other town in the country! There is a vast network of traffic-free cycle tracks through parkland, around lakes, along canal towpaths and disused railways. It is also at a crossroads of the National Cycle Network: Route 51 passes through Milton Keynes on its way from Oxford to Cambridge, whilst Route 6 runs south from Derby down to the River Thames at Windsor. This ride described below starts on the western fringes of the town, at the old bridge over the River Great Ouse between Old Stratford and Stony Stratford, running alongside the river for four miles on a tarmac path. You pass through a narrow tunnel through the Iron Trunk Aqueduct carrying the Grand Union Canal over the River Ouse then beneath the railway viaduct. At New Bradwell the route veers away from the river and joins the course of the dismantled railway through leafy cuttings as far as Newport Pagnell.

BACKGROUND AND PLACES OF INTEREST
The Ouse Valley Park
Forming part of Milton Keynes' extensive system of parks, the Ouse Valley Park runs east from Stony Stratford for 5 miles. Although the park is crossed by three major transport routes (the A5, the West Coast mainline and the Grand Union Canal) it still has a rural atmosphere with old parkland trees and hedgerows providing refuge for wildlife. The River Great Ouse flows from North Oxfordshire to the Wash.

Grand Union Canal
The Grand Union Canal, or Grand Junction Canal as it was called until 1929, was built between 1793 and 1805 to link London with Birmingham. The lowest point between the two summits at Braunston and Tring was at the crossing of the River Ouse. The canal authorities decided to build the Iron Trunk Aqueduct to carry the canal over the valley and thus avoid the need to construct several locks. Watermills have probably stood by the River Ouse at Stony Stratford and Wolverton since at least Domesday.

Starting Points & Parking:
1. Old Stratford/Stony Stratford – from the roundabout at the junction of the A5, A508, and A422 to the northwest of Milton Keynes, take the exit towards Old Stratford and Stony Stratford, cross the bridge over the River Ouse then take the next right signposted 'Stony Stratford Centre' and park along this road.

2. Newport Pagnell – start from the car park at the junction of Marsh End Road, Wolverton Road and High Street. Take Marsh End Road, signposted 'Ousedale Centre' then turn first right by traffic lights (between a car dealers and an off licence) signposted 'Milton Keynes Railway Walk'.

ROUTE INSTRUCTIONS:

1. Start from the bridge over the River Great Ouse on the road between Old Stratford and Stony Stratford (southeast of the roundabout at the junction of the A5/A508/A422). TAKE CARE crossing the road via the traffic island onto the path signposted 'Wildlife Conservation Area, Canal, New Bradwell'.

2. Stay close to the river (on your left). After almost 1 mile, go through a metal gate, turn left and then shortly, at an offset crossroads with a wide track/drive (there is a large red-brick house to your left), go straight ahead onto a continuation of the path. Go through a narrow tunnel beneath the Iron Trunk Aqueduct (carrying the Grand Union Canal). There are some steps down the other side.

3. Cross a wide wooden bridge over a side stream and turn left at the T-junction signposted 'Riverside Walk, New Bradwell' to pass beneath the massive brick railway bridge. After almost 1 mile, at a fork of tracks immediately after crossing a small bridge over a stream bear right away from the river signposted 'National Cycle Network Route 6'.

4. Follow NCN 6 signs, running alongside a main road (V6), under two large, closely spaced concrete bridges then turn sharply left, signposted 'Railway Walk, Newport Pagnell'.

5. Join the railway path (near Bradwell Windmill) and follow signs for 'Newport Pagnell'. Cross the Grand Union Canal after 1½ miles. Stay on the railway path for a further 2 miles. The trail ends at Sheppards Close in Newport Pagnell.

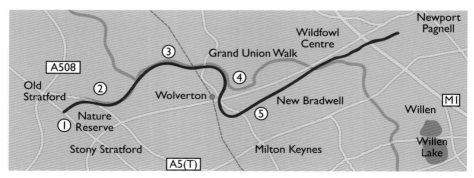

Distance: 11 miles one way, 22 miles return.

Map/leaflet: Ordnance Survey Landranger map 152. Far more useful is the Milton Keynes Redway Map, showing the vast network of cycle lanes in the area (see website below).

Website: www.mkweb.co.uk/cycling is an excellent website with plenty of interest for every sort of cyclist. You can also download the Redway map for free.

Hills: None.

Surface: Tarmac or good stone-based tracks with a couple of short rougher sections on the northern part of the ride between Great Linford and Cosgrove.

Roads and road crossings: One short section on road in Great Linford to visit the Nag's Head pub.

Refreshments: Nag's Head pub, Great Linford. New Inn (Bridge 72). Galleon pub, Old Wolverton. Barley Mow pub, Navigation Inn, Cosgrove.

This ride gives you a real idea of how much work has gone into the creation of the Redway in Milton Keynes. At one extreme, running 4 miles north from Woughton on the Green in the heart of town, you have the Broadwalk, one of the finest examples of landscaped, tree-lined, traffic-free cycle trails in the country; at the other end of the spectrum are stretches of the canal towpath lying outside the town boundaries where no improvement work has been undertaken and the rough surface means that your bones and bikes will get a good shaking. Luckily these rough sections are a rarity. There is much to enjoy on this ride, from the aforementioned Broadwalk to the wide grass expanses of Great Linford Park, the lovely old buildings in Great Linford itself, the rural vistas as the canal passes out into the countryside and the long mural of a freight train with its diverse load on the canalside wall in Wolverton. Cosgrove is a small attractive village with two pubs and makes a convenient turn around point. This being Milton Keynes, there are plenty of options for varying your return journey although it is recommended you carry a Redway map with you (see previous page).

STARTING POINT & PARKING:

The car park on Newport Road, Woughton on the Green, on the east side of Milton Keynes (Grid reference SP 877382).

ROUTE INSTRUCTIONS:

1. From the entrance to the car park in Woughton on the Green, turn left then right at the road hump onto the yellow gravel track on the other side.

2. Continue in the same direction through parkland ignoring several left turns until arriving at a red-brick humpback bridge over the canal (Bridge 87). Turn right on the Broadwalk, keeping the canal to your left.

3. Continue north along the Broadwalk parallel with the canal for 3½ miles following signs for Woolstone, Newlands and Willen Park. Keep an eye out for the bridge numbers. At Bridge 78 B (a new bridge with metal railings), the main wide path swings up and to the right, turning back on itself to cross this bridge over to the west side of the canal. Remember this point for the return trip.

4. Proceed north alongside the canal for ⅓ mile then just before a red-brick bridge at a 4-way signpost turn left: 'Linford Manor Park'. At a crossroads of paths go straight ahead 'Playing fields' then cross the road onto High Street.

5. As the road swings left by the Nag's Head pub turn right through gates into parkland. Pass between old houses, go past the church then a collection of large stones. Rejoin the canal towpath, which shortly changes sides.

6. Follow the canal over a variety of surfaces for a further 4½ miles to Cosgrove, passing the following landmarks: New Inn (Bridge 72), a long black and white mural with pictures of freight trains, the Galleon pub, the Trunk Viaduct over the River Ouse, the junction with the Buckingham Arm and the Navigation Inn and Barley Mow pub at Cosgrove.

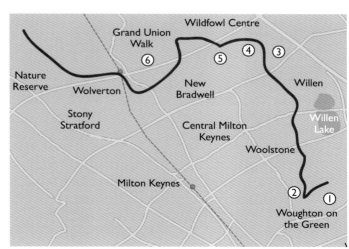

ROUTE 22
From Bedford to Sandy

Distance: (a) 7 miles from Priory Country Park east to the A1 near to Sandy (14 miles return). (b) 3 miles from Priory Country Park west to the end of the riverside path, beyond Bedford County Hall (6 miles return).

Map/leaflet: Ordnance Survey Landranger map 153. See also *Cycle Map – Bedford and Kempston* produced by Cycling Campaign for North Bedfordshire (www.ccnb.org.uk).

Website: www.sustrans.org.uk

Hills: None.

Surface: Good stone-based tracks, tarmac.

Roads and road crossings: If you choose to go right into the centre of Sandy you will need to use a mixture of roads and cycle paths to the east of the A1. Heading west, there is a toucan crossing of the busy Prebend Street (bridge) by County Hall.

Refreshments: Lots of choice in Bedford and Sandy. The Priory Marina pub in Priory Country Park (Bedford). The Crown pub at Willington. Cafe at the Danish Camp.

Cycle Hire: Priory Marina Cycling in Priory Country Park (01234 340090).

Starting from the attractive setting of Bedford's Priory Country Park with its marina, lakes, the River Great Ouse and a bike hire outlet, the course of the old railway whisks you east towards Sandy across a landscape of rich arable fields. Shortly after crossing the bridge over the A421 you have the option of following a direct route along the railway or taking a longer route alongside the River Great Ouse. Both join at the cafe at Danish Camp, a fine stopping point with lovely views out over the river. Another attraction along the way is the Dovecote at Willington. The railway path continues to the edge of Sandy, just west of the A1. The route into town from here uses a mixture of cycle paths and residential roads so you may prefer to turn around at the end of the traffic-free section. Heading west from Priory Country Park there is an attractive riverside route right through the centre of town.

BACKGROUND AND PLACES OF INTEREST
Bedford
Bedford's prosperity dates from the late 17th century when the River Ouse was made navigable to the sea and the town became an important point for distributing goods up and down the river. During the 18th century a network of turnpike roads radiated out from Bedford and during the first half of the Victorian period the railways arrived in the town.

Starting Point & Parking:
Priory Country Park, to the east of Bedford town centre, signposted off the A428 Bedford to Cambridge road (Grid reference TL 073494).

ROUTE INSTRUCTIONS:

East from Priory Country Park to Sandy

1. From the marina in Priory Country Park follow signs for 'Willington' 'Sandy' 'National Cycle Network Route 51' and 'Danish Camp' along the course of the old railway. The cycle path runs on a yellow gravel path parallel to the service road.

2. After 1½ miles cross the bridge over the A421 dual carriageway. Shortly you have a choice to reach the cafe at Danish Camp, via the direct route or the riverside route. Both are attractive: why not try one on the outwards trip and the other on your return? If you wish to visit Willington Dovecote and the Crown pub in Willington, take the direct route.

3. Both routes rejoin at Danish Camp. Beyond here there is a short narrow section of footpath where you will need to walk. Signs indicate the start and finish of this section.

4. If you are with children it is suggested you turn around after a further 3 miles at the end of the traffic-free section immediately before the A1 dual carriageway bridge. However, if you wish to go on into Sandy there is a waymarked 1.4-mile route mainly on cycle paths and residential roads into the centre of town where there are plenty of refreshments.

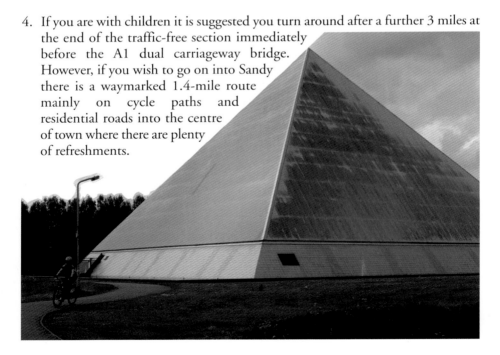

West from Priory Country Park through Bedford
Following 'Town Centre' signs, there is an attractive riverside path west from Priory Country Park into the centre of Bedford (by County Hall) along the south side of the river then after crossing the main road bridge via a toucan crossing, along the north side of the river for a further mile. You may wish to go and see the extraordinary Sikh Gurdwara Temple in Queens Park.

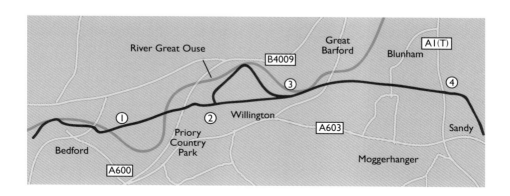

ROUTE 23

Cole Green Way west of Hertford

Distance: 4 miles one way, 8 miles return.

Map: Ordnance Survey Landranger map 166.

Website: www.welhat.gov.uk > Leisure > Cycling and Walking

Hills: None.

Surface: Good stone-based tracks. The woodland section near Hertford may be muddy in winter.

Roads and road crossings: None, unless you choose to continue west on National Cycle Network Route 61 into Welwyn Garden City from the end of the trail or to go east to link to the Lee Navigation through the centre of Hertford.

Refreshments: Lots of choice in Hertford, Cowper Arms pub at Cole Green, about halfway along the route.

This short, attractive railway path connects the western edge of Hertford with the eastern edge of Welwyn Garden City, passing under a vast railway viaduct near to the start at Hertford Football Club then running though a cutting with overarching broadleaf woodland forming a canopy over the path. The first half of the ride is primarily woodland and pasture, the western half is more open with more arable fields, although there is a large plantation of broadleaf woodland just beyond the subway beneath the A414. Your only chance of refreshment on the route itself is at the Cowper Arms pub near Cole Green. However, the National Cycle Network route through the centre of Hertford to the start of the Lee Navigation is fairly quiet and takes you past some fine cafes with outside seating so you may choose to add this on to the main route.

BACKGROUND AND PLACES OF INTEREST

The old railway line

The Cole Green Way follows the course of the old Hertford, Dunstable & Luton line. It was opened in 1858 and carried passengers up to 1951 and freight until 1962. It was acquired by Hertfordshire County Council in 1974 and converted to recreational use

Hertford

Little remains of the old Norman castle except the lovely 15th century gatehouse. This was one of the childhood homes of Elizabeth I. It was near to Hertford in 1712, in a village called Walkern, that the last trial for witchcraft ever held in England took place. As a result of the case, the barbaric laws relating to witchcraft were repealed.

Starting Point & Parking:

In central Hertford, turn off the A414 by the Gates Ford dealers onto West Street, signposted 'Hertford Town FC'. On a sweeping left-hand bend about 300 yards after the Black Horse pub bear right, signposted 'Cole Green Way, Welwyn Garden City' and park by the football ground (Grid reference TL 321121).

ROUTE INSTRUCTIONS:

1. From the Hertford Football Club car park aim towards then pass beneath the large railway viaduct. After 200 yards bear right at a National Cycle Network Route 61 sign staying on the broad gravel track through woodland.

2. Go past a car park on the right. Exit here if you wish to visit the Cowper Arms pub.

3. Pass through the subway under the A414. Climb past the recently planted woodland on your right.

4. The traffic-free trail ends after a further mile at a T-junction with a road on the eastern edge of Welwyn Garden City (at the junction of Black Fan Road with Cole Green Lane). NCN 61 continues on a mixture of quiet streets and cycle paths into Welwyn.

East from Hertford FC car park
A well-signposted route on quiet streets leads through Hertford town centre to the start of the Lee Navigation towpath near to Hartham Leisure Centre.

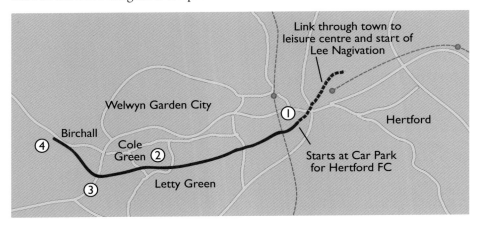

ROUTE 24
From Hertford to Waltham Abbey along the Lee Valley

Distance: 14 miles one way, 28 miles return from Hertford to Waltham Abbey. This is a ride which can be as short or as long as you like. There are several pubs along the way which you may choose as turnaround points.

Map/leaflet: Ordnance Survey Landranger map 166.

Website: www.leevalleypark.org.uk and follow links to 'Cycling' or www.waterscape.com

Hills: There are no hills.

Surface: Good quality gravel track.

Roads and road crossings: Care should be taken crossing the road in Ware – follow the signposted cycle crossing. There is another narrow but busy road to cross just south of Dobb's Weir.

Refreshments: Lots of choice in Hertford. Lots of choice in Ware. Jolly Fisherman pub, Crown pub south of Ware. Rye House pub, Rye House. Fish & Eels pub, Dobb's Weir. Lots of choice in Waltham Abbey.

Cycle Hire: Lee Valley Cycle Hire, Old Mill and Meadows, Broxbourne 01992 630127 or 07949 768249

This superb open section of canal towpath is one of the best in the region. The whole Lee Valley has become one of the finest areas for recreational cycling to the north of London. The ride described here follows the Lee Navigation from its northern terminus in Hertford eastwards through the attractive town of Ware before taking a southerly course through to Waltham Abbey. This is just a suggested turnaround point; you may wish to push on further and link with Ride 25 south from Waltham Abbey all the way into London, joining the Thames near Limehouse Basin!

BACKGROUND AND PLACES OF INTEREST

Ware

From the Middle Ages corn and malt were transported from Ware to London by river. Once the second largest malting centre in the country and known as the granary of London, Ware had 22 maltings in 1788.

Starting Point and Parking:

The long stay car park near the swimming pool/leisure centre on Hartham Lane, Hertford. From the centre of Hertford follow signs for the B158 (Parliament Square roundabout, The Wash, Millbridge) past the library then turn right onto Hartham Lane past Hertford Brewery to the car park. The car park is free at the weekends.

ROUTE INSTRUCTIONS:

1. From the Hartham Leisure Centre in Hertford follow 'National Cycle Network Route 61, Ware' signs on the cycle path across the recreation ground, cross Bridge 69 over the canal by the lock keeper's cottage and turn left along the towpath of the Lee Navigation.

2. After 2 miles, at the road junction in Ware at the end of the towpath, bear right and use the traffic islands (take care) to cross the busy road straight ahead to rejoin the towpath.

3. Follow this excellent towpath for 5 miles to the Fish & Eels pub at Dobb's Weir. Beyond here the path quality varies: parts are excellent but there are also some short rougher stretches.

4. After 1½ miles go past the Lee Valley Boat Centre and the Crown pub.

5. Continue for a further 6 miles to Waltham Abbey. You will know you are here as it is just after Waltham Town Lock, at Bridge 42. It is suggested you turn around at this point but you may wish to link with Ride 25 to continue south into London.

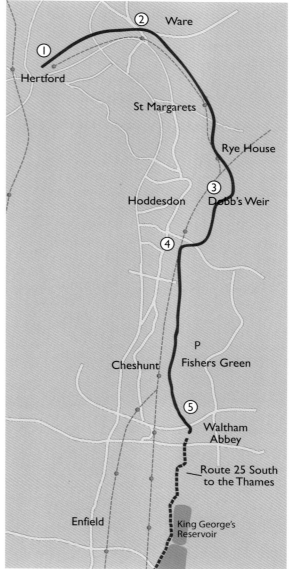

Distance: 14 miles one way, 28 miles return.

Map/leaflet: Ordnance Survey Landranger maps 166 and 177 although more useful is a London street map or the *Lee Valley Regional Park* map (see website below.

Website: www.leevalleypark.org.uk and follow links to 'Cycling' or www.waterscape.com

Hills: None.

Surface: Good stone-based tracks, tarmac.

Roads and road crossings: The occasional road crossing, none dangerous

Refreshments: Pubs at regular intervals all the way along the towpath. Stonebridge Lock Cafe, Tottenham. Springfield Park Cafe, Upper Clapton.

Cycle Hire: Lee Valley Canoe & Cycle Centre, Stonebridge Lock, Tottenham 07747 873831

Linking Islington in central London with Waltham Abbey in Hertfordshire, the Lee Navigation is a green corridor offering one of the best escapes from city to country. At the southern end there are several canals: the Regent's Canal which emerges from Islington Tunnel is part of the Grand Union Canal, leading to its junction with the Thames at Limehouse Basin (the western junction of the Thames and the Grand Union Canal is at Brentford); the Hertford Union Canal links Regent's Canal with the Lee Navigation alongside Victoria Park and then there is the Limehouse Cut. North of Hackney/Stratford and the Olympic Zone there is just the Lee Navigation, winding its way north past Hackney Marshes with their hundreds of football pitches. The path is wide and there are no low bridges, by contrast with the route in London itself. To look at the map one would imagine seeing a succession of vast reservoirs up the valley. As it is, the towpath lies below the surrounding embankments for the reservoirs and they remain hidden. There are lot of pubs and a couple of cafes along the way so you have plenty of reasons for taking this ride at a leisurely pace.

NB In London along the Regent's Canal the towpath is narrow under the low bridges – ring your bell, slow down and be prepared to give way when you meet people. This section is popular both with walkers and cyclists.

BACKGROUND AND PLACES OF INTEREST
Limehouse Basin
Originally called Regent's Canal Dock, Limehouse Basin is where the Regent's Canal meets the Thames. In the 19th century this provided access to sea-going vessels trading from all over the world. The original Thames Lock separating the Thames and the Basin was large enough to allow ships into the basin where they could unload their goods onto canal boats. A smaller lock replaced the original in 1989. This was due to the decline in ship trade and the need to save more water.

Victoria Park
In 1840, a petition was sent to Queen Victoria, signed by 30,000 residents, urging the formation 'within the Tower Hamlets, of a Royal Park'. Work began in 1845 and was completed in 1850.

Starting Points & Parking:
1. Waltham Abbey - the best car parks for the canal towpath are signposted just to the north of the town, either at the Royal Gunpowder Mills (Grid reference TL 377010) or a little way north along the B194 at Fishers Green (Grid reference TL 376027). Another option is at Enfield Lock just south of the M25.

2. Islington, London – at the east end of the tunnel, at the junction of Noel Road, Danbury Street and Graham Street (Grid reference TQ 316834).

ROUTE INSTRUCTIONS:

1. From Waltham Abbey follow the towpath south, with the canal to your left. Pass under the M25, go past the Greyhound pub then Enfield Lock.

2. After 6 miles you will come to the Stonebridge Lock Cafe by the Lee Valley Canoe & Cycle Centre.

3. After a further 2 miles there is another cafe at the north end of Springfield Park.

4. Go past the hundreds of football fields that cover Hackney Marsh.

5. About 12 miles south of Waltham Abbey, and just south of Hackney Wick, you will need to turn off the Lee Navigation onto the Hertford Union Canal to continue south to Limehouse Basin or west to Islington on Regent's Canal. This point is by the Olympic site, marked by a 3-way sign. You need to turn right here, signposted 'Hertford Union, Victoria Park'.

6. Pass alongside Victoria Park then at the T-junction* with Regent's Canal you can:

(a) turn left for 1½ miles to Limehouse Basin and the Thames

(b) turn right for 2½ miles for Islington, as far as the tunnel (at the junction of Noel Road, Danbury Street and Graham Street).

Remember this point for your return trip as it is easy to miss.

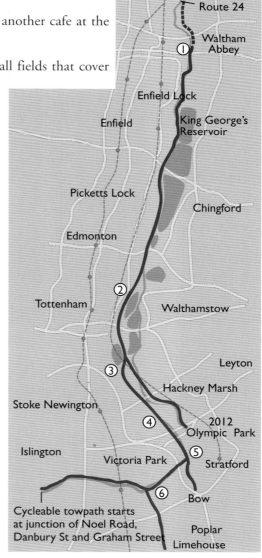

95

ROUTE 26
A Circuit in Epping Forest

Distance: 8-mile circuit.

Map/leaflet: Ordnance Survey Landranger Sheet 167 or 177. Better still are the larger-scale maps that can be purchased from the Visitor Centre at High Beach which show the trails in much greater detail.

Website: www.cityoflondon.gov.uk and put 'Epping Forest' in the 'Search' box.

Hills: There are several short hills, some of which are quite steep.

Surface: Good quality gravel tracks, although these may become muddy in the depths of winter or after prolonged rain.

Roads and road crossings: Great care should be taken crossing the roads, particularly the A104 and A121. Allow yourself time to gauge the speed of the traffic and wait for a clear gap in both directions.

Refreshments: King's Oak pub and cafe at the start.

Although there is no specifically waymarked bike trail in Epping Forest there is such a plethora of top grade gravel tracks that it would be possible to make up lots of routes criss-crossing this ancient woodland, owned and managed by the Corporation of London. The ride starts from the King's Oak pub in the heart of the forest and wastes no time before diving into the wooded delights on a broad gravel track. Great care should be taken on the crossings of the busier roads but in general as long as you are prepared to wait for a clear gap in the traffic, the roads should not deter you from exploring Epping Forest's fine network of tracks. It is notoriously difficult to give woodland instructions so do not get exasperated if you think you are lost! The most important point is that you are outside cycling in beautiful woodland, you will never be that far from where you started and if you take a different route from the one described, it is not the end of the world, is it?

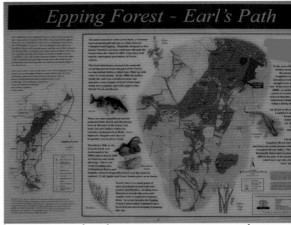

BACKGROUND AND PLACES OF INTEREST

Epping Forest

This public open space is owned and maintained by the Corporation of London. Its 6000 acres are a mixture of ancient woodlands, heaths, bogs, ponds and grassy plains. More than half the area is a Site of Special Scientific Interest in recognition of the Forest's unique stands of old pollarded trees and their associated wildlife.

Starting Point & Parking:

The King's Oak pub at High Beach, near the Visitor Centre in the middle of Epping Forest. This is located about 1 mile northwest of the Loughton/High Beach roundabout on the A104, the road running north from London towards the town of Epping (Grid reference TQ 412980).

ROUTE INSTRUCTIONS:

1. With your back to the King's Oak pub by the High Beach Visitor Centre turn right. At the T-junction (with a gravel parking strip opposite) turn right then left onto a track by a barrier and wooden posts. At a second road go straight across 'Emergency Access'. Ignore a left turn after 150 yards.

2. At the busy A121 go straight ahead (TAKE CARE) then shortly at a T-junction of tracks turn right. At the next major track junction, with a tall wooden fence ahead and a metal barrier across access to the road to your right, turn left.

3. Cross a minor road (there is a 'Give Way' sign to the right). The next ¼ mile is noisy, running parallel with the B1393. Cross this road straight ahead. At a T-junction after 300 yards (with silver birches to your left) turn right.

4. Go through car parks either side of the B172 and past a 'Jack's Hill' signboard. Easy to miss: after ½ mile, on a gentle descent, take the first broad track on the right. Descend then climb. Go through a car park and diagonally left across the busy A121 (TAKE CARE).

5. Follow another downhill stretch, climb up through a car park and cross the road past a pond. Go past a second pond then after ¼ mile, on a gentle descent shortly after a large grass clearing on the left, take the next right by a white post with a horseshoe sign.

6. Cross the busy A104 (TAKE CARE), go through a bridlegate then turn right on a minor road (this is a no through road, without traffic). At the T-junction (with a car park and tea hut to the right) turn left then right onto a broad track with 'Emergency access' barrier.

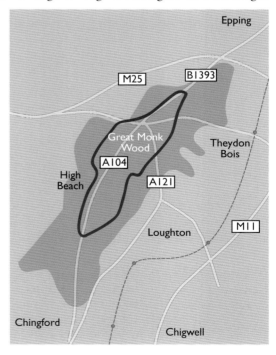

7. Lots of ups and downs. Ignore a right turn on a wide track by a small triangle of grass with trees in it. At the T-junction with the next road turn left to return to the King's Oak pub/Visitor Centre.

ROUTE 27
Flitch Way, from Braintree to Great Dunmow

Distance: 7½ miles one way, 15 miles return.

Map: Ordnance Survey Landranger map 167.

Website: www.essexcc.gov.uk and type 'Flitch Way' into the 'Search' box.

Hills: None.

Surface: Good stone-based track, tarmac. If you go on through Great Dunmow to the western part of the Flitch Way the surface is much rougher.

Roads and road crossings: One road crossing near the old Felsted Station. You will need to use quiet lanes to access the Flitch of Bacon pub in Little Dunmow and busier roads if you choose to go into Great Dunmow.

Refreshments: Lots of choice in Braintree. Tearoom at the old station at Rayne. Flitch of Bacon pub, Little Dunmow. Lots of choice in Great Dunmow, just beyond the western end of the ride.

This wide railway path has been improved over the years and offers an easy flat ride through the gently undulating Essex countryside. The trail starts conveniently from the railway station car park at Braintree, soon passing the handsome old buildings of Rayne Station, which is now a tearoom. A long footbridge over the new A120 takes you high above the traffic and back onto the wooded corridor leading westwards. There is one point (near the old Felsted station) where a bridge has been removed and you need to descend to the road before rejoining the path. Unfortunately the railway path does not continue into Great Dunmow, so you can either turn around at the end of the traffic-free section (perhaps visiting the pub in Little Dunmow) or if you are happy to negotiate the traffic of Great Dunmow, to link with the western half of the Flitch Way which runs from the B1256 to the west of the town for a further 6 miles to Tilekiln Green, just east of M11, Junction 8. Be warned that parts of this are rougher and finding the Great Dunmow start is not easy (it is at Grid reference TL 623216).

BACKGROUND AND PLACES OF INTEREST
The old railway line
The Bishop's Stortford to Braintree branch line, a single-track railway, opened in 1869. Farmers and local industries made much use of the railway to transport goods to and from the main towns. The small tank locomotives that worked the line became part of everyday life. The passenger service was closed in 1952 but steam, and later diesel locomotives continued with goods traffic until the line finally closed in 1969.

Why the Flitch Way?
The name comes from the famous medieval Flitch Ceremony, held in the village of Little Dunmow. This ceremony was originally set up by the local Augustinian monks. It involved giving a flitch (a large piece of bacon) to couples who had not argued in marriage after a year and a day.

Starting Point & Parking:
Braintree railway station (Grid reference TL 762227).

ROUTE INSTRUCTIONS:
1. Follow through the overflow car park (furthest from the railway station) to the start of the Flitch Way. The surface is at first tarmac.

2. Cross a bridge over a road then after 1¼ miles there is a chance of refreshments at the old station at Rayne. Shortly cross a long bridge over the new A120.

3. After 3¼ miles and shortly after a 'Felsted Station' signpost, descend to the road, cross to the pavement opposite, turn right then left up a flight of steps. At the tarmac turn left then right onto a continuation of the railway path, passing above a travellers' site.

If you wish to visit the Flitch of Bacon pub at Little Dunmow, immediately after passing under the next bridge turn right, then at the lane turn left and follow this road (Brook Road) into Little Dunmow, turning left at the T-junction for the pub.

4. The railway path ends after a further 1½ miles where National Cycle Network Route 16 is signposted off to the right. You can continue into Great Dunmow following NCN 16 signs although this will involve using busier roads.

NB There is a second stretch of the Flitch Way to the west of Great Dunmow although the surface is at times a lot rougher. It starts off the B1256 on the southwest edge of town at Grid reference TL 623216.

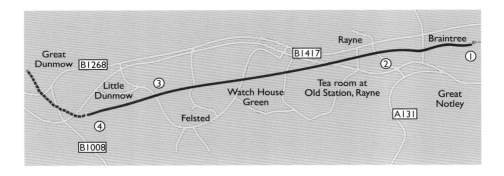

ROUTE 28
The riverside path between Colchester and Wivenhoe

Distance: 5 miles one way, 10 miles return from Colchester Leisure World to Wivenhoe.

Map/leaflet: Ordnance Survey Landranger Sheet 168. There is also a Colchester Cycle Map available from Colchester Tourist Information Centre (01206 282 920) or see the website below.

Website: www.essexcc.gov.uk and type 'Colchester Cycle Map' into the 'Search' box.

Hills: None.

Surface: Tarmac or good quality tracks.

Roads and road crossings: Two busy roads are crossed safely via toucan crossings. The only street which may carry any traffic is Hawkins Road on the industrial estate between the two traffic-free sections. The roads near to Wivenhoe Quay are very quiet.

Refreshments: Rose & Crown pub, Station pub, Tudor Tearooms, Wivenhoe. Lots of choice in the centre of Colchester.

This ride links two clusters of beautiful old buildings, one in the very heart of Colchester and the other around Wivenhoe Quay, via a mixture of quiet streets, paths through parkland and (for the greater part of the ride) a traffic-free riverside path along the River Colne from the southeastern edge of Colchester past the University of Essex to Wivenhoe railway station. It is well worth going beyond the station to explore the quay and pubs by the riverside in Wivenhoe. For those of you looking for a totally traffic-free ride it would be best to start at Wivenhoe station and turn around at the end of the cycle path after 3 miles. However, if you are prepared to use some short sections on quiet streets you soon join another traffic-free stretch alongside the river and through parkland, arriving right in the heart of Colchester's historic city centre.

BACKGROUND AND PLACES OF INTEREST
Colchester
This ancient town stands on the site of the Roman city of Camulodunum which was founded in AD 50. The huge keep of the Norman Castle, which was built on the base of the Roman Temple of Claudius, houses a collection of Roman antiquities.

Starting Points & Parking:
1. Colchester - Leisure World/Ten Pin, just south of Cowdray Avenue, the A133 Colchester Bypass (Grid reference TM 001260).
2. Wivenhoe - the railway station car park, 3 miles southeast of Colchester (Grid reference TM 037216).

ROUTE INSTRUCTIONS:

1. Start at the Leisure World/Ten Pin Bowling car park. Follow the tarmac cycle path (white line down the middle) directly away from the Ten Pin Bowling soon passing a 'Wivenhoe Trail' sign. Cross a bridge and turn left, keeping close to the water on your left following 'Wivenhoe Trail' signs through the parkland.

2. Cross the busy road via toucan crossing. Pass between allotments and past metal sculptures. Briefly join road. Cross a bridge and turn left onto Hawkins Road through industrial estate.

3. Immediately before the roundabout cross the road to join a cycle path. Use the toucan crossing to cross this very busy road.

4. Follow the riverside path for 3 miles, passing the University of Essex up to your left. The trail passes through woodland with the railway to left and the river to the right and emerges at Wivenhoe station.

5. It is worth exploring the riverfront along Old Ferry Road and maybe taking refreshments at the Tudor Tea Rooms, the Station pub or the Rose & Crown pub.

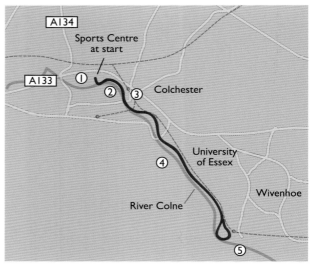

ROUTE 29
A Circuit of Alton Water south of Ipswich

Distance: 8-mile circuit.

Map/leaflet: Ordnance Survey Landranger 169 or there is an A4 leaflet available from the Visitor Centre or Cycle Hire Centre which shows the lanes in the immediate vicinity and the location of the pubs.

Website: You can download a copy of the Alton Water map from www.altoncyclehire.co.uk/images/altonmap2.jpg

See also www.anglianwaterleisure.co.uk

Hills: There are a few short hills on the north side of the lake.

Surface: Mainly good quality gravel tracks. Some short, rough sections on the north side of the lake.

Roads and road crossings: There is a very short section on road, crossing the bridge at the western end of the lake.

Refreshments: Cafe at the Visitor Centre. White Horse pub, Tattingstone White Horse. Wheatsheaf pub, Tattingstone. Kings Head pub, Stutton. The Compasses pub, the Swan Inn, Holbrook.

Cycle Hire: At the Visitor Centre (01473 328873).

This fine reservoir circuit is being improved a little more each year, making the route safer and easier with each improvement. Alton Water is also popular with water sports so on fine, breezy days you will catch sight of windsurfers racing each other across the lake with their bright sails skimming over the surface. Although this is a relatively easy and flat ride you should be warned that there is a (short) hillier and rougher stretch on the north side of the lake between Birchwood car park and Lemons Bay. You may prefer to follow lanes for this section (maps showing the route plus the surrounding lanes are available from the cycle hire centre). There is a cafe at the Visitor Centre and lots of pubs just near the route so you could either follow the circuit close to the lake itself or make this part of a longer ride exploring some of the beautiful and quiet lanes on the Shotley Peninsula.

BACKGROUND AND PLACES OF INTEREST
History of Alton Water
During the 1960s, it became clear that Ipswich would need new sources of water supply and the Tattingstone valley was chosen as the location of a new reservoir. Work started on the dam in 1974 and the 390-acre, 2,000-million-gallon reservoir was completed in 1976. Its name derives from Alton Hall, which now lies beneath the water.

Starting Point & Parking:
The Alton Water Visitor Centre, off the B1080 between Stutton and Holbrook, 6 miles south of Ipswich and 4 miles east of the A12 at Capel St Mary (Grid reference TM 156354).

ROUTE INSTRUCTIONS:

The route is well signposted.

1. From the Visitor Centre keep the water to your right and follow the numbered waymarkers for the Alton Water Circuit clockwise around the lake.

2. After 3 miles, at the road, turn right over the bridge then right again through the car park onto a gravel track, following the bike route signposts. Certain sections on the north side of the lake are a bit rough and there are some steeper climbs and descents.

3. Cross the dam and follow the lakeshore round to the right back to the start.

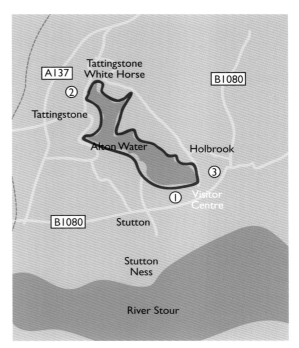

ROUTE 30
Rendlesham Forest

Distance: 6-mile circuit for the yellow trail and 10-mile circuit for the green trail.

Map: Ordnance Survey Landranger map 169. A *Rendlesham Forest* leaflet is available by calling the forest centre (01394 450164).

Website: www.forestry.gov.uk/rendlesham

Hills: One gentle hill towards the end.

Surface: Good stone-based tracks.

Roads and road crossings: None.

Refreshments: None at the centre, the nearest are in Butley or Hollesley.

There are two family cycle trails starting from Rendlesham Forest Centre. The short trail, waymarked yellow, is approximately 6 miles long with a shortcut allowing you to halve your ride. The long trail, waymarked green, is 10 miles in length. Both trails are off road on sand, gravel and grass. The rides pass through mixed woodland and clumps of bright yellow gorse. For a section of the route you are right alongside the perimeter of a disused airfield with large round hangars.

NB Cyclists are requested to respect both the wildlife of the forest and its visitors. Please give way to walkers and horse riders, and do not cycle through plantations. Also please avoid cycling on the main picnic areas and the 'Easy Access' walking trail.

BACKGROUND AND PLACES OF INTEREST
UFO sighting
The Rendlesham Forest Incident is the name given to a series of reported sightings of unexplained lights and the alleged landing of an extraterrestrial spacecraft in Rendlesham Forest in December 1980. It was never taken seriously by the Ministry of Defence but it has had sufficient impact for the Forestry Commission to waymark a 'UFO' trail in the woodland!

Starting Point & Parking:
The entrance to Rendlesham Forest is accessed via a minor off the B1084 to the east of Woodbridge, northeast of Ipswich (Grid reference TM 355484).

ROUTE INSTRUCTIONS:
The route is very well signposted and there are too many turns to give junction-by-junction instructions. The short trail (yellow waymarks) and the long trail (green waymarks) both start from the main car park by a large signpost with 'All trails start here'. It is also possible to join the trail at several other points, for example from other car parks on the approach road to the main car park.

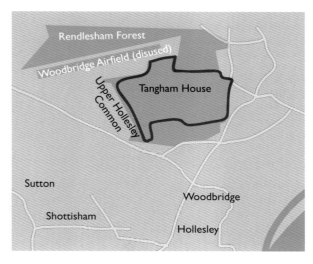